THE POOR CATHOLIC

The Road to Grace

Angelo Paul Ramunni

Grace Path Publications
Canaan, Connecticut

THE POOR CATHOLIC: *The Road to Grace*
First edition published by Grace Path Publications, LLC, 2004.

Grace Path Publications, LLC
P.O. Box 898
Canaan, CT 06018
(860) 824-0506 (phone and fax)

SAN: 256-2332

ISBN 0-9761766-0-2

Library of Congress Catalog Number: 2004112990

Manufactured in the United States of America

Cover design and text layout by Carleton M. White
of Ellington Printery, Inc., Ellington, Connecticut

Printed in the United States of America
Grace Path Publications, LLC
P.O. Box 898
95 Main Street, 2nd floor
Canaan, Connecticut 06018
(860) 824-0506
www.thepoorcatholic.com

10 9 8 7 6 5 4 3 2 1

This book is dedicated to all of you who have been seeking a life of peace, happiness and joy. Perhaps without even knowing it, you have been searching for God and to people like you Jesus said,

Come to me, all you that are weary and are carrying heavy burdens, and I will give you rest.

MATTHEW 11:28

It is my hope and prayer that you find peace and a renewal of your spirit in the words that follow. May you also find your way home to eternal life with the Lord as you read and live out his words each day.

And this is eternal life, that they may know you, the only true God, and Jesus Christ whom you have sent.

JOHN 17:3

CONTENTS

Preface ix
Introduction 1

PART I: STARTING OUT AS A YOUNG CATHOLIC

1. Some Things We Just Don't Talk About 13
2. The Early Years: Growing Up as a Catholic 31
3. Life Before *In His Steps* 51

PART II: TIME SPENT WITH GOD

4. Life After *In His Steps* 59
5. Nice Story, But It's All Optional, Right? 71
6. Learning to Walk with the God of the Universe 81
7. The Bottom Line Scriptures: The Core of God's Message 95
8. The Real Bottom Line 97
9. Speaking Directly 105
10. How Then Should We Live? 107
11. Going Home 111
12. It's About Children 115
13. Please Bring Them Home 121
14. What to do About Sin 125
15. The True Nature of Sin 133
16. Praying in the Lap of God 137
17. *Ora Labora* 141
18. Pray Without Ceasing 145
19. Interceding for Others 147
20. How We are to Treat Others 155

PART III: CHALLENGES TO OUR FAITH WALK

21. The Barriers to Living Out Our Faith: A Personal Testimony 167

PART IV: FINDING OUR WAY HOME

22. The Bottom Line Question: "Am I Getting into Heaven or Not?" 215
23. The Road to Grace: The Way to Get Home 231
24. Closing Thoughts 257

Notes 269

Acknowledgements 271

About the Author 273

PREFACE

Wouldn't it be wonderful to know without a doubt what heaven is all about? Wouldn't it make our lives so much easier? It would help remove the anxiety and uncertainty many of us feel concerning our eternal futures and regardless of how tough things may get in this life, we could always confidently look forward to that day when we would enjoy eternal peace, forever.

There are many places a person can go to discover how things will be in the afterlife. The problem with many of these sources is that they are based on someone's thoughts and ideas that may not necessarily be rooted in the spiritual truth of the Scriptures. And since many of these sources come from people, aren't they speculative at best? Consider this: if we want to know more about our future eternal home, don't we need a reliable spiritual source to inform us?

The twenty-first century has just begun and already we are faced with an important series of additional related questions including:

- Who will be the source of all truth in this new millennium?
- Where can we go as Roman Catholics and Christians to secure truthful answers about all of the difficult questions we are encountering every day?
- When our children, friends, family members, co-workers, and others ask us important life questions, whom shall we quote or to what source can we direct them?
- Who can consistently tell us what is right and what is wrong in all cases?
- Does such a source even exist any longer?

For Catholics, the standard answer to these questions would refer us back to the tenets of the Roman Catholic Church as expressed in the catechism. But if one looks at the behavior of Catholics as a whole over the past forty years or so, it becomes obvious that many Catholics do not agree with a good number of the teachings of the Catholic Church and even with the statements of the Pope himself.

So I would suggest that we backup to the first question of all spiritual questions and decide whether we believe there is a God or not. If there is not, then the source of all truth must come from a natural or human place, namely people.

At this point we must look to people such as our government leaders, educators, the media, the state police, the IRS, the FBI, the court system, and similar organizations to tell us what we should believe and what we can and cannot do.

But if there is a God—the God of the Bible and the Christian faith—then it makes every bit of sense to look to Him as the source of all truth. If He truly does exist, then He must be the cause of all that we know and experience. As the Creator of all things, He would be the very best source from whom to seek answers. Since God would be our one and only supranatural source, logically His wisdom would "trump" the wisdom of any person or body of people.

I have written *The Poor Catholic* in the hope that people will understand that it is the God of the Bible who holds all answers (both temporal and eternal) for us. Without any doubt, I have found this to be very true in my own life.

More and more Catholics today are leaving traditional ways of thinking and behaving behind them, and are trading those ways for new untested theories about life and personally attractive lifestyles.

Proof of this movement is readily available in every news report and via every media outlet. Ironically, the many people who still hold to traditional morals and values have chosen to largely remain silent in the defense and promotion of these time-honored ideals. Their silence has only served to help promote the growth of this trend away from God.

Now more than ever we need to rediscover the home base for

all truth. It's not only that we no longer agree on the issues, but more importantly, we no longer agree on the principles. The core values and foundational principles that helped establish our nation and even our Christian faith have changed, at least from an application point of view. Whatever has replaced those values has taken root in too many peoples' thoughts and lives. *The Poor Catholic* will help redirect your attention to the one reliable source of truth and salvation, which is found in the Trinity of God the Father, God the Son, in the form of Jesus Christ, and God the Holy Spirit.

Since the 1960's, it seems that we in our American culture have decided that truth can be discerned and developed by and for each person.

In this new age, we each have the ability to create our own personal truths with which we can live our lives. Truth no longer springs from an absolute source. It comes from each person as they deal with their desires and perceived needs. We also have the ability to modify those truths to fit our needs of the moment, which might differ significantly from the needs of just the day before. Truth for this new era is very personal, conveniently adaptable, and very anti-absolute in nature.

For Catholics especially, the loss of absolute truth has been most unsettling. This fact alone can account for the "drift" of Catholics away from the core values of their Christian faith, and it has left countless people in a moral and spiritual vacuum. Many of us grew up learning and believing in God as the absolute source of all truth and all that is good. The world is now demonstrating that this foundational belief has changed and is no longer true. Consequently, many issues in society, both at the local and the national levels, are becoming nearly impossible to solve. In some cases, compromise can still settle certain problems, but the parties involved will likely see it as a setback since their personal truths did not prevail, and they will carry the memory of that to the next issue they confront.

They may eventually yield in future cases, but it is likely they will do so grudgingly and without a sense of love or concern for the greater good of the community. Yielding in successive issues and contests will therefore become more and more unlikely.

When truth springs from an individual and personal source, we end up with as many versions of truth as we have people. While this may work in the privacy of our own homes, it will create great strife and disagreement when experienced in a public setting. Relatively common tasks, such as driving a car, can become very dangerous. For example, people may begin to determine for themselves what the speed limits should be and whether or not they will stop at red lights or stop signs. What will we do then?

There are no different versions of the truth. All truth that does not spring from the same source will compete and eventually collide. It will create chaos and if left unchecked could lead to anarchy. And in the spiritual world, there is nothing worse than anarchy.

Beyond these issues, there lies the greatest of all threats, which should concern even the most nominal of all Catholics and Christians. If there is a God who controls all things temporal and eternal, then ultimately it is He whom we will have to deal with in the end. If we believe in an afterlife, then there must be a border between this life and the next. What will you do when you get to that border? Who will you find there in charge of the border crossing? Who will you gamble on meeting—Jesus Christ or the god of your own personal truths? What will happen when you find out it is the God of the Bible who controls the afterlife and entrance into it? It will be at this moment when His truth will prevail over our own self-created truths. *The Poor Catholic* lays out many of the eternal truths given to us by God in the hope that you, the reader, will allow God to convince you *now* of their veracity and applicability to today.

As you read this book, please keep these thoughts in mind. I believe you will find answers to many questions as you move along. I hope you will also find in this book the encouragement to seek out the one true God, His Son Jesus Christ, and His Holy Spirit.

Not only will you discover them to be the source of all truth, but you will realize this fact with the aid of a most special tutor, the Holy Spirit. As I put this book together, it is my personal prayer that the Holy Spirit will accompany every copy that's printed and act as a tutor to all who read it. I pray that the Holy Spirit will help you truly seek to know God in order to develop a close personal walking faith with His Son, Jesus Christ. In this way, when you arrive at the border, Jesus will already recognize you and you Him. At that point, crossing into eternal life will be an easy task.

If you commit to read this book slowly and thoughtfully, with the intention of becoming God's disciple (student), you will begin to receive answers to many of your questions, such as the ones we spoke of earlier. He will reveal to you truths that concern not only this world but also the next.

With many such parables he spoke the word to them, as they were able to hear it; he did not speak to them except in parables, but he explained everything in private to his disciples.

MARK 4:33-34

INTRODUCTION

When you think about it, of all the things we can desire most in life, eternal life should be at the top of the list. But it is an odd thing about human beings—most of us do not actively pursue a place in the hereafter. Instead much of our daily efforts go toward acquiring things that make our present lives more comfortable. It just doesn't make any sense. Our lives on earth last for only eighty or ninety years at most, but eternity is forever. So, shouldn't we be more concerned with our eternal welfare?

Few of us realize a very simple but profound fact. God Himself wants the same thing that every willing person on this earth wants for himself or herself. We both want eternal life. God wants us to be home with Him for all eternity, and I think this is also something we each would want the most. This of course makes sense only to those who believe in God. If you have no belief in the existence of God, then this life is all you have. If this is as good as it gets, you need to take advantage of every opportunity while you can.

But salvation can be a tricky thing for us to understand and capture for ourselves. Our way of living today places little or no value on the prospect of a life after death. Most of us spend no time and energy in trying to see what God has planned for us after we die. I guess we feel that in the end He'll somehow work out the details and so we personally don't have to be concerned about it right now. Think about it. Do you know of anything else in your daily life that happens successfully without any planning, forethought, or concern from us? I know of nothing.

Salvation does not occur for us simply because we want or expect it to happen. It happens because we come into agreement with God on how we want to spend not only our eternal lives, but even more importantly, our lives here and now.

Why is this life more important? Because this is where we can have the greatest impact for God's kingdom, right here on this earth and in the lives of those around us. Once we get to Judgment Day, all of our opportunities to make positive changes will be gone.

Once we agree with God that we want eternal life for ourselves, then both God and we go to work on it jointly. That's right: we cannot receive eternal life if only God wants it for us. Similarly, we cannot obtain it all by ourselves through our own efforts. Interesting, is it not? The God of the Universe cannot alone give us eternal life unless we first accept it and then work it out with Him in this life. He will never force it upon us. We cannot earn it, nor can we expect to just sit back with arms folded and see God carry us through the gates of heaven. No, we must first *agree* to walk through those gates on our own, and then we must follow through with the promise.

God did His part to help make heaven available to us. The death of His only Son on the cross re-opened the gates to heaven, and Jesus also keeps those gates open for us even to this day. God even sends His Holy Spirit into this world as we live and work, to help influence and encourage us as we find our way home. The key to eternal life, then, is that we must work closely with God every day. As Saint Paul said:

> *Therefore, my beloved, just as you have always obeyed me, not only in my presence, but much more now in my absence, work out your own salvation with fear and trembling.*
>
> PHILIPPIANS 2:12

Our goal as Catholics should be to get ourselves home to be with the Lord. On that last day, what could be more important than to find ourselves on the *inside* of the great doors to heaven?

Many Catholics have not fully appreciated and understood what is involved in the process of salvation. As I said earlier, some people think that somehow, God will do it all for us, and there are others who believe they can work their way into heaven. Sadly, both positions are very wrong.

Our salvation is a process of love, work and friendship with the God of the Universe Himself. As you will read in this book, we must first begin to build that relationship—what I call "a walking faith with God." Everything else arises from this bond. The more we look for it and nurture it every day, the stronger it grows and the more likely that marvelous things will occur because of it.

Jesus knew His mission on earth was to rescue humanity from the kind of eternal existence we would have without God. His whole effort was directed at saving us and making certain that we would have every opportunity to find our way home. He worked very hard to put into plain words how we are to think and behave in our daily lives. He also revealed what God wants from us on a personal level.

It's unusual to think about what God would want or need from *us*, but there is one place in particular where Jesus revealed His deepest desires and concerns for us. In the seventeenth chapter of the book of John, just before Jesus' Passion and death, the Son of God prays for His disciples and all those who would follow Him in the future. It might be said that these are Christ's last words to His Father about us, and for that reason alone they become extremely important. Read now a few of the verses from that prayer and feel the passion and concern Christ has for each of us:

> *Father, it's time.*
> *Display the bright splendor of your Son*
> *So the Son in turn may show your bright splendor.*
> *You put him in charge of everything human*
> *So he might give real and eternal life to all in his charge.*

And this is the real and eternal life:
That they know you,
The one and only true God,
and Jesus Christ, whom you sent.
I'm not praying for the God-rejecting world
But for those you gave me,
for they are yours by right.
I'm saying these things in the world's hearing
So my people can experience
My joy completed in them.
I'm praying not only for them (His disciples)
But also for those who will believe in me (us today)
Because of them and their witness about me.
The goal is for all of them to become one heart and mind –
Just as you, Father, are in me and I in you,
So they might be one heart and mind with us.
Then the world might believe that you, in fact, sent me.
Father, I want those you gave me
To be with me, right where I am.

JOHN 17:1-3, 9, 13, 20-21, 24, *The Message*, emphasis added

Much of what Jesus prayed for in John 17 is what we discuss here in this book. Jesus was asking His Father not only on behalf of His Disciples but also everyone else ever born as well. This prayer teaches us that salvation is not a singular event. By that I mean that your salvation and mine involve those around us as well. As we get saved and prepared to meet God in heaven, this process should also impact the people we live and work with, if we allow them to share in our experience.

We also need to realize that at the center of Jesus' prayer is His knowledge that there is a great ongoing battle between the forces of evil and God's Kingdom over the soul of every person created by God. Satan's job is to populate hell. On the other hand, God's utmost desire is for all of His children to return home to live in peace and happiness with Him for all eternity. Whether or not he or she realizes it, the "Poor Catholic" is someone who is given a choice to follow Christ each day.

We as poor Catholics, or even poor Christians for that matter, are caught in the middle of this great struggle and we must choose which side to join every day. We must awaken to the reality that God is waiting for us to make the choice to either walk with Him or walk our own way. If we choose to follow along with Him, we will store up many riches in heaven and in this way we will no longer be poor. Instead, we will become rich in God's eyes.

Jesus of course knew this and took every opportunity to tell those in His day (and us today) what they needed to do. His prayer in John 17 is strictly for those who have not rejected God and all that He stands for.

He also prays that we will all unify and become of one heart and mind and in this way be in agreement with Him and His Father. Finally, Jesus then makes the ultimate request. He asks His Father to allow those who follow Him to be with Him forever in heaven.

The sense we get from studying this prayer of Christ is that anyone who does not choose to follow Him will be poor indeed—because he or she will have failed to see what God values most in our lives. Jesus considers successfully loving God and all those we encounter each day to be our most precious achievement. Failing to understand this will produce for us an eternal future that will be dismal at best.

The Poor Catholic, then, focuses on what awaits all of us in the future. The message is one that no one can afford to ignore. The absolute worst thing that could happen to a person is that he or she dies in ignorance about eternity and the process of salvation. That should happen to no one.

This book also helps us see what God is expecting from us. It is a call to all Catholics and Christians to return to their spiritual roots and rediscover what is so special and sacred about the God many of us learned about as children.

Some Further Thoughts to Consider

This would be a good time to clarify a few things before we go any further. First, my personal journey has *not* taken me to a place where things are now very clear and easy to understand. My walk has led me "further up the mountain" to a higher vantage point where I can see certain things more easily. But if anything, my challenges are greater now than ever before and require a greater commitment from me.

Second, you will see throughout this book references to the holy Scriptures, the Roman Catholic catechism, and other reliable sources. I include these not only to help frame the discussion but also as reference for your own research, which I heartily encourage. After all, Scripture is one of the prime ways that God communicates with us as He did personally in the Old Testament, and then through the words of His Son in the New Testament and subtly by the Holy Spirit throughout the entire book. When we begin to look for Him, He will come to us through His words in the Bible. So, when looking for God, we must first go back to His original words, and the circumstances under which He said them so there can be no misunderstanding of what He said and meant.

Additionally, reading the Scriptures gives the Holy Spirit the opportunity to have a "personal impact" on you. He will come as you read and you will feel His influence, just like someone who studies with a private tutor. This kind of encounter can be most profound and life-changing.

Remember also that the words of the Bible are themselves sacred and therefore most powerful. As Catholics, many of us have never gotten comfortable with reading Scripture directly from the Bible. Yet, if you plan on nurturing a "walking faith" with Christ, then reading and meditating on the word of God, directly from the Bible, is an absolute must. It is my hope that you will begin to acquire this habit as you read through this book (if it isn't already your daily practice).

Third, this is not an effort to reform or repair today's Catholic Church. The Church, just like any large organization, always needs improvements and changes in its operation. However, any comments I make here regarding the Catholic Church are simply offered as personal observations from a Catholic who has arrived at a certain level of faith with God. And that faith is based solely on one important person, Jesus Christ.

As a matter of fact, one of my goals in writing this book is to help Catholics, as well as other Christians, wake up and see Jesus. *He is real.* The curious thing about this statement is that as Catholics we are all supposed to believe this fundamental fact: Jesus is really present here in our world, as He is, for example, in the Holy Eucharist during Mass.

But our actions in all matters of life and especially in our relationships with people rarely reflect that belief. In fact, they usually reveal a *lack* of faith in God's existence or His ability to help us. For example, when we seek answers to our financial problems, we typically look to those touted as professionals or experts in the field of financial services, thinking that they must have the answers we need. It could be. But my experience has taught me that, more often than not, our problems have resulted because we have pursued our own desires without considering what is truly best for us, that is, what God wants for us. A financial consultant is unlikely to advise you of that fact.

We must first look to what God is saying through the abundance of what we have or our lack of resources. There's always a message from Him, and there's always an eternal impact for each of our everyday actions. God is real, and since we spend so much of our time pursuing wealth and personal gain, He can and will speak to us through the things that consume the majority of our attention. Remember: *He will find us in the place where we spend most of our time and deal directly with us there.*

The fourth point is this: time seems to be passing more and more quickly these days. As it says in Isaiah 55:6, *"Seek the LORD while he may be found, call upon him while he is near."*

See the wisdom in this verse. While God is not planning to leave us, it's very possible that we might soon be leaving Him. As we concern ourselves more and more with earthly matters of money and personal gain, it is possible to unconsciously turn away from God and move further and further from Him, even though we may not have meant to do such a thing. So while He is still near and you still have the time and ability, go to Him and find out what He wants from you personally.

Finally, I'd like to emphasize that what follows is a personal record of the path I have taken to finding God in my own life. I have been—and I still am to a certain degree—the "Poor Catholic" discussed in this book. I know without a doubt that I have been on a road filled with His graces in my walk with Him. I have kept a prayer journal where God answered many critical and personal prayers. There could be no other explanation other than God's intervention, for how things turned out in my life. Some of what follows could be embarrassing for me, but I offer these stories and thoughts in the hope that they could possibly help you find God in your own life.

Please note that since it is a major premise of this book that we should first and foremost love God, I have decided to capitalize all words and names used in reference to God and the other members of the Trinity. I hope this will serve as a reminder as to the proper way of beginning a new love relationship with God. We need to first show our reverence and respect for Him even in how we address Him or think of Him.

The message of this book is presented in four parts:

Part 1 touches on my childhood and talks about what it was like growing up as a Catholic. Many readers will no doubt recognize familiar themes.

Part II covers my time spent with God after His presence finally became a reality to me. We discuss what I call the "Bottom Line Scriptures" that are fundamental to our faith as Catholics.

Part III addresses the difficulties we all encounter in living out our faith, especially in the workplace. We will discuss whether having a faith that we don't exercise in public is useful or useless.

Part IV is perhaps the most important section of the book: it covers the big question of what it will take to move from being a poor Catholic to being one who is rich in God's eyes and thereby ready to receive eternal life.

As John 17 clearly indicates, Jesus is in charge of all things relating to us and He alone has the power to grant us eternal life. But think about it. The whole purpose of Jesus the person and Jesus the Son of God, is that He died in order that we could return to be home with His Father. Jesus, His Father, and the Holy Spirit want nothing more and nothing less than that for us. *The Poor Catholic* offers you a way to become an answer to those very prayers of Jesus Himself.

Taste Them Again for the First Time

Not too long ago, a well-known cereal company faced a dilemma when they found that their sales of cornflakes were dropping off after many years of solid market share. With so many new, sweeter, and more attractive cereal options on the market, management had to develop a new approach to selling their old standby product.

Using clever television ads, they showed middle-aged people eating cornflakes. While re-discovering how great-tasting a simple bowl of cornflakes was, the people remembered how good and uncomplicated their childhood years had been. The ads ended with the tag line, "Taste them again, for the first time."

So in a similar manner, let's take a fresh, new look at the God of the Bible. Many of us grew up with some form of religious instruction and for some reason may have either left that training or modified it beyond recognition for our own purposes. Why not try to find the God we once knew as a child and reconnect with Him? The good thing about where we are right now is that we have tried and experienced a number of alternative possibilities and solutions to cure what ails us. In all of that experience, it doesn't seem as if anyone has found a better way to solve our problems.

I ate lots of cornflakes as a child, and I remember liking them very much. While we still have the opportunity, let's take time out, sit down, and, as if we were children once more, "taste them again maybe for the first time."

PART I

STARTING OUT AS A YOUNG CATHOLIC

1

Some Things We Just Don't Talk About

One of the unique features about *The Poor Catholic* is that we will be discussing topics that are not freely talked about in our normal conversations with one another. Questions like whether there is a God, an afterlife, the existence of places such as heaven and hell and other similar notions are seldom talked about openly. Exactly why this happens is truly a mystery, especially when you consider how important these topics are to us. But I do have a theory about this.

I believe we do know the answers to some of life's big questions, or at least we strongly suspect we know. There is something built into us that innately knows the truth about these questions. The best way to describe it is to call it a "spiritual instinct." And because of this instinct, we already know more about God than we are willing to admit publicly and perhaps even to ourselves.

This creates a problem for us. Because if we start to research and discuss the details surrounding these questions, we might find out for certain what we suspect to be true. And what do we suspect? In truth, we know there is a God and we know that He expects us to live a certain way. The problem is that we fear that we'll find out for sure that God does not approve of the way we are living and this means we must change our ways in order to be in compliance with His laws. And the one thing we absolutely hate to do is change from having things the way we like them. But for us in this book, we will not let this deter us in our search for the truth.

Since we will begin our search by discussing the key question of how a person can gain eternal life, it makes sense to first ask an important related question: Have you ever wondered who's in charge of eternity?

If there's a heaven—and it seems that most of us believe there is—then it stands to reason that some "entity" needs to be responsible for how things work there. Is it God? Is there a God? Again, most people believe that there is a supreme being called God. Then isn't it logical that He would be responsible for managing heaven, as well as things in this life? It follows that He would also be the one who determines who gets in and who does not. Think about it. If He's the gatekeeper, then doesn't it make sense that we live our lives in such a way as to meet His requirements for entrance into heaven?

A few years ago, a movie came out called *Independence Day*. It told a story about a powerful race of aliens that came to take over earth. They positioned huge spaceships—each probably ten to fifteen miles in diameter—over many of the world's major cities. For a while, they just hovered in the sky as the people below wondered what they were going to do. Later, when the aliens were asked directly what they wanted of us they replied, "We want you to die."

Seeing this scene brought to mind a similar situation that has existed even up to the present day. God is real and like those spaceships, He too hovers above, around and near us.

In the movie people couldn't avoid seeing the spacecraft. They had to stop what they were doing and deal with the aliens. But for us, it's easy to ignore God's presence. He doesn't impose

Himself on us. He patiently waits for us to acknowledge Him and then He responds. Those of us who do notice Him will ask what He wants of us, and His answer will be as different from the aliens' answer as can be. God says to each of us, "I want you to live. Follow me."

The great unspoken question before us then is whether or not we truly believe in the existence of the God of the Bible. Is He here or not? If He is, then do we accept His word as law? And furthermore, even though we may not agree with some of His laws, are we willing to comply with all of them, as He requires? Or do we believe only in the rules we agree with or like? To the extent we do this, we will have created our own god. This is what is called creating an idol, something God is very much against.

This kind of god may serve us well here in this life, but it would be foolish to bet on him helping us in the life hereafter. For all of us Christians, this turns out to be the biggest silent issue before us in the twenty-first century.

So the question becomes, which god or God controls eternity? On which one will you place your bet? Each of us goes to our grave betting on one or the other because we will have lived our lives according to the rules of one or the other. The next question then, is this: which god or God did you actually follow? We'll find out only on the Day of Judgment whether we followed the right one or the wrong one.

If you watch the news these days, you'll see story after story of people in bad, often life-threatening situations. As a society we are terribly confused by these events and we seldom seem to agree on the proper way to live in order to avoid such situations. We no longer know what is correct behavior or wrong behavior. Not knowing which god or God to follow affects our judgment and our behavior and can lead us into troubling situations.

It's as if we've lost our moral compass or our moral direction, which should always point us toward the one true God.

Consequently, we can no longer see what is right and what is wrong. Public opinion polls often reveal a population split down the middle on issue after issue. This is symptomatic of a culture that has lost its understanding of God. Consequently, we might as well flip a coin in order to decide how to correctly deal with a problem, no matter how serious. Actually, it's quite simple. If God is the source of all good, then isn't it logical that we seek Him out for help and answers to all our problems? After all, don't we always want only what is best for all concerned regardless of the problem?

If God is not the only possible and reliable source for a correct sense of right and wrong, then who else can tell us consistently and accurately what is right and what is wrong? Once we eliminate our one and only supernatural source, then all we have left to rely on is a human source. And as we know, we humans are not perfect. So whom should we listen to? Whose values should we make our own? If we agree that it is God who we should listen to, then the question arises of whether we actually know Him or not. Many of us do not have a correct understanding of God and His ways. What is worse, we seemed to have lost our fundamental ability and desire for having even a simple conversation with one another about God.

Everything in our culture today points to the truth of these facts. In my estimation, these are the foremost questions facing us, not only in the Catholic Church today, but in all of Christianity. A good proof of this is that many people seem to believe that on the day of final judgment, God will accept whatever belief system we've constructed for ourselves and applied in our own lives. This must be true because so many of us can no longer even agree on many of the fundamentals of our Christian faith. Yet, if we are to base our faith on the Scriptures, then this kind of thinking is definitely wrong. The Israelites tried to live this way many times in the Old Testament and the results for them were disastrous. If we truly knew God and understood what's at stake, then we would not be changing and customizing His laws to fit our particular needs. We would instead accept His word for what it is—the truth—and live by it every day. As Saint James tells us in his letter to the early Christians, *"But be doers of the word, and not merely hearers who deceive themselves"* (James 1:22).

He did not say to be doers of our own word or to be doers of the Word as we interpret it. God wants us to do specifically what His Word says, with no alterations, modifications or interpretations. But to do His Word, we need to understand who and what God is all about. We must never forget that God is the one constant in our universe. Everything else will pass away except Him and He has not and will not ever change. Remember this:

> *Jesus Christ is the same yesterday, and today, and forever.*
>
> HEBREWS 13:8

As Catholics, many of us have not put any real time and effort into finding out who God is and what He expects from each of us on a personal level. For example, many of us expect that He'll automatically grant us heaven when we pass on. Why should He do that? What has He said in Scripture that gives us such a right to enter heaven? Have we lived our lives in accordance with His instructions or mainly in accordance with our own desires?

On this point alone, we need to be absolutely certain if we expect to gain eternal life. Each of us needs to prayerfully consider this matter to his or her own personal satisfaction and security. We cannot and should not be taking anyone else's word for it. Where we will spend eternity depends largely on whether we understand what God is all about and what He's been saying to us on a personal level. Remember, He is in charge of eternity.

What is a "Poor Catholic?"

In the introduction to this book, I gave an overall reason for the poorness of Catholics and Christians in general. To reiterate, there is a tremendous invisible conflict occurring every day as the forces of heaven battle against the forces of hell over the salvation of our souls. Catholics and Christians are caught in the middle and would be considered merely as pawns in this struggle if it were not for the fact that we have free will. This means that each of us gets to choose which side we will follow every day.

We probably do not think of it this way but in truth, this is how God and Satan both experience it, and that makes it a reality. Actually, it's a form of reality that exists beyond our natural abilities and senses—a struggle that originates in a spiritual realm and plays out here in our world. Many times the occurrence of good and evil events in our lives attests to the realness of this struggle.

Again this is one of those things that we just don't like to think about or discuss. It reminds us of just how fragile and vulnerable we are. In the Introduction, you read Jesus' words in John chapter 17 and you saw His personal concern for us. If the Creator of all things knew we'd all end up in heaven with Him in the end, then why is He that concerned for our eternal welfare? His words prove that we need to do what we can now to be ready to meet Him. In the end you will see that because of this eternal life and death struggle, being close to Jesus is the only safe place to be in this life. Since this is the case, *The Poor Catholic* will take you on a journey that is headed straight toward Jesus Christ. He is our destination and shelter.

But the concept of being a poor Catholic goes even further. Most dictionaries, in their definition of the word "poor" will include the word "lacking." If a person is poor, they will most probably be lacking things such as financial and other personal resources.

For our purposes here, a Catholic might be considered poor if he or she lacked an adequate knowledge of God or did not have a personal walking faith with God. The poor Catholic could also be someone whose faith and prayer life is more casual or passive in nature rather than active and vibrant. In any event, the core of the concept is that we've lost that critical element or part of a relationship that creates a successful link with God. We've lost something of great value and that something is a knowledge and love of Jesus Christ on an intimate and personal level.

Even as I wrote this book, people asked me about its title. As soon as they hear those three simple words, "The Poor Catholic," they respond with "Oh yes, that's a perfect title!" Why is that? They have no idea what the book is about but the name already means so much to them. The answer is simple. There are many Catholics, all of whom can personally relate to the title. Instinctively, they know that they lack something very important in their faith walk and they are profoundly aware of it.

They can be active or non-practicing Catholics, former Catholics who've left the Church, former clergy, converts from Catholicism to another faith, abused Catholics and many, many others. All of these people share one common characteristic: *they miss their relationship with Jesus Christ in the context of their Catholic Church.* For so many, it makes no difference where they have gone. For them, there is still the haunting absence of that peace and security they once knew and learned about while growing up as children in the Catholic faith. And now many want it back again.

Many of these people didn't want to leave their Church or stop practicing as Catholics, but they did for one reason or another. I cannot address all these issues here, but I can tell you what the universal solution is for each one. It is developing a personal knowledge of Jesus Christ. I know you've heard this before, but I have found that there is healing for all that ails us in

His words and in His arms. We are one of God's most fragile creations. We are easily hurt, insulted, emotionally and psychologically scarred and we may feel physically at risk much of the time. God knew this when He made us and He could have made us tougher. But He didn't. Do you know why? So we would need Him and those around us to survive. God's favorite mode of operation is to get us to work together. His two greatest commandments, loving God and one another, prove that point. *He wants us to lean on Him through those whom He places nearest us.*

The poor Catholic comes in many different forms, shapes and sizes but in every case is damaged in some way and is in need of healing and love. Even more, a person is at their poorest when they don't even have an awareness of their need for a close, loving, personal knowledge of God. Sadly, many go through life this way thinking it is normal.

So where does a person turn? When a person has been seriously hurt by someone, it is possible that the fabric of their soul has been damaged or torn; the hurt can be that deep. All too often we think that a doctor or some medication will fix what ails us. For sure, professionally treating our medical issues is highly recommended. But we often cannot see the spiritual tear inside of that person's being and there is only one place to go to repair that kind of hurt. We must go to the Father much like a child who turns to his or her earthly parents and guardians when in trouble.

We can access God through those around us, but I have found that it is so important that we first go to God directly. A friend may give us too much sympathy, poor advice or even criticism instead of the real help we need at that moment. Meeting God in His Holy Scriptures can open our eyes and it gives God a chance to talk to us directly. Think of God as being your own personal emergency room. Once the immediate care is given, then the long-term care we may need can come through those He places around us. The main point here is this: stay close to Him always. When you have a concern, you just simply need to turn to Him and He will be there.

Consider this: if Jesus were to appear here on earth again just as He did 2000 years ago what would He say to people? Do you think He'd have anything new to tell us? Do you think His original instructions found in the New Testament are missing something? Or would all of His "current advice" be the same as found in the Bible? I think you know the answer to this question.

My point is simple. We already have the answers to the problems that plague us. We just refuse to study His Word where those answers are found and talk about it with one another. Think of it this way. The words of Christ found in the four Gospels are the foundational principles of our Catholic faith. As we start to invest a little time in reading and understanding these words, God sends His Holy Spirit to act as a tutor, if you will, who will help us apply those principles to our particular situation. The principles themselves actually become the tools we use to construct the answers we need and the Holy Spirit helps us accomplish the task.

It is my hope that you will see throughout this book different ways you can approach God with your questions. I have found that it is best to approach Him like a small child would, with trust and sincerity (see Matthew 18:1-5). Go to Him with no preconceived notions or agendas and most importantly, with an open heart. He will always be ready to work with you to make things better.

I remember what a good friend advised me once when I was going through a tough time in my life. He said, "God rarely airlifts you out of the hole you've gotten yourself into, but He will support you as you climb out." That was marvelous advice and I have found it to be so true.

As you make your way through this book, you will find numerous quotes from Scripture that will strongly encourage you to get closer to God both in knowledge and in practice. In later chapters, I will discuss how to love God, how to love others, how important children are to God, and other topics. Again these are all things that we normally don't talk about with one another but they are important issues. And we'll be studying them from God's point of view, which will make it even more interesting.

A New Old Tool – "The Road to Grace"

Many of the discussions that follow are designed to help you overcome being a poor Catholic. One of the more meaningful ways I've chosen to accomplish this is by using a concept called the "Road to Grace."

Think of the Road to Grace as a pathway to God. When a person decides to follow Christ, they literally agree to do things in their daily lives that please God. In essence, they look to live their lives as Jesus would.

This might sound daunting to many of you, but in reality it's not that complicated or difficult to understand. When we choose to walk with God, we step onto a path where we literally look for God in the everyday occurrences of our lives. When He sees our intention is to come toward Him and to get to know Him better, He sends His grace to encourage and support us in the effort. The further we travel along this path, the more grace He extends to us.

Perhaps you now can start to see the link between the poor Catholic, someone who is lacking in personal knowledge and experience with God and the Road to Grace. It is upon this road that the things we are lacking are given to us. If we remain on this path we will eventually find our way home to be with God in eternity. This road is the only sure path I know of that will ultimately lead to eternal life.

However, I would caution you not to think of this path as some kind of automated walkway to an easier life, and eventually heaven. It is definitely not that. If we believe in an all-powerful, all-knowing, ever-present, loving and just God, then that belief is justified only if we act as if God is here and involved in our lives. Our job every day is to dedicate all of our efforts toward pleasing God just as we do for those around us whom we love. We must choose to act in a Christian manner as we interact with people at work, at home, or anywhere else.

We can best accomplish this task if we decide to step onto the Road to Grace, and the sooner we decide to do so, the better. Additionally, it's while walking on this road you will likely experience something called rebirth or conversion. In time, enough of God's grace will come to us and we will be transformed (born again) by the experience. Here's how Saint Paul put it:

> *Do not be conformed to this world, but be transformed by the renewing of your minds, so that you may discern what is the will of God—what is good and acceptable and perfect.*
>
> ROMANS 12:2

A good example of how we do conform to the ways of this world is by not talking to others about something as important as coming to God. These are critical issues for us because they deal with our eternal salvation. If we refuse to work on this with those around us, then heaven will elude us in the end. But when appropriate, if we bring these issues to the forefront of our conversation with others, all will gain in the end. In the process we will learn how to comply with Romans 12:2 as our minds, hearts and souls will be transformed to eventually look like the mind, heart and soul of Jesus Himself. This book will not only help you on your journey to God but it will also provide you with a roadmap for how you can continue to walk toward God and find Him, even if you have to do this on your own.

Make-Believers

It's truly ironic. We worry about terrorist attacks and weapons that can snuff out our lives in a matter of seconds. But somehow we don't seem to be concerned about whether we will gain eternal life. What causes this? Is it arrogance? Smugness? Or is it due to a severe case of ignorance or apathy concerning the truths about eternity?

Whatever the case may be, it proves that we as a society just do not understand how God works and we are doing little or nothing to find out. What is worse, we are doing this to our children as well. This is more dangerous than any terrorist attack or nuclear threat because it involves not only our eternal disposition but also theirs. Someone once explained the problem to me in a very interesting way. He said, "On the one side you have all the believers and on the other side you have all the non-believers and in the middle, you have a huge group of make-believers."

The make-believers are usually well-intentioned people. They come from all walks of life. But they all share one common characteristic: they are poor (lacking) in their personal knowledge of Jesus Christ. Or more insidiously, they have over-analyzed God and His words to such an extent that their interpretations of the Scriptures no longer bear any resemblance to what God originally meant. Left uncorrected, either of these tendencies will ultimately lead to one's eternal separation from God.

We know that "make-believe-ism" is a disease that's not only widespread in our culture today but also in Christianity itself. In a way, it has developed as a form of self defense. It's how many of us end up dealing with unpleasant news or events. We simply act as if it didn't occur or we can ignore it since the news will not affect us personally.

This may work for certain things in our lives but for something as important as our eternal life, we cannot afford to bury our heads in the sand. If we do, we are in essence ignoring what God is saying to us. We refuse to see the truth of how we are living in relation to Him. It is a chief reason why so many of us are poor in God's eyes. What's worse, we do not even realize it! Saint John expressed this truth very clearly in the book of Revelation:

For you say, "I am rich, I have prospered, and I need nothing." You do not realize that you are wretched, pitiable, poor, blind, and naked.

Revelation 3:17

If this Scripture doesn't alarm you, then little else in God's Word will move you to get right with Him. It sums up many of the "big silent issues" we've just discussed, even though we may not be aware of their importance or existence. The health of our relationship with God and the people around us, our core beliefs and God's value system are more of those secret and unspoken issues we should be concerned about. If our concern is real then it should move us to take action on all of these items. As Revelation 3:17 indicates, God's attention is on the things that we seldom focus on.

Throughout my years in school, I remember sitting in class after class listening to my instructors emphasize certain points. I paid attention and took notes on those points. Why? Because I knew that if they were important to the teacher, then they would probably be on the upcoming exam. And they always were. It's no different a situation when dealing with God. He is speaking and we need to listen.

From time to time, many of us must wonder if there is a

possibility that we will not make it into heaven. What follows is a line of thinking that represents the greatest threat a make-believer could possibly face one day. Let's look at the following statements and see if we can develop an answer to the question that arises at the end of this line of reasoning. Remember, to arrive at the correct response, we must think of it as it would appear from God's point of view:

- You were born a Catholic and baptized into the Catholic Church.
- You made your first Communion and received your Confirmation.
- You were married in the Catholic Church and raised your children as Catholics.
- You went to Church most Sundays and holy days and, from time to time, even went to Confession.
- You supported your Church financially.
- And now you've just had a beautiful Catholic funeral and you expect to enter heaven.

So, are you really sure God will let you in?

This list of statements seems complete, doesn't it? It sounds like this person complied with Church law and the rules of our faith as found in the catechism. So what could possibly be missing? Is there any way this person could be found at fault? To find the correct answer, take a look at the following Scripture verses:

A certain ruler asked him, "Good Teacher, what must I do to inherit eternal life?" Jesus said to him, "Why do you call me good? No one is good but God alone. You know the commandments: You shall not commit adultery; You shall not murder; You shall not steal; You shall not bear false witness; Honor your father and mother." He replied, "I have kept all these since my youth." When Jesus heard this, he said to him, "There is still one thing lacking. Sell all that you own and distribute the money to the poor, and you will have treasure in heaven; then come, follow me." But when he heard this, he became sad; for he was very rich.

LUKE 18:18-23

We, like the person in these verses, are asking the same question. We've kept all the Commandments, we've gone to Church every week, we've frequented the Sacraments and in general, complied with most of the published rules and laws of the Church. So what else could there be to do? But to Jesus, these things by themselves are not enough.

He wants each of us to get rid of anything that prevents us from making Him the center of our lives. He also wants us to provide for those in need. Most importantly, He wants us to follow Him. In other words, He wants us to get close to Him and develop that close personal walking faith with Him. Again, look at this key verse of Scripture:

And this is eternal life, that they may ***know*** *you, the only true God, and Jesus Christ whom you have sent.*

JOHN 17:3, emphasis added

Jesus is telling us that the key to entering heaven is to know Him, not just corporately as we do at Mass, but also in a personal way. On that last day, He will not judge us as a group, but rather each of us individually, one by one (see Ezekiel 18:30). Knowing Him then as you would a close personal friend will be critical, as Jesus points out in these following verses:

Then I will declare to them, "I never knew you; go away from me, you evildoers."

MATTHEW 7:23

Later the other bridesmaids came also, saying, "Lord, lord, open to us." But he replied, "Truly I tell you, I do not know you."

MATTHEW 25:11-12

Going even further, if we look at another special verse in the book of Revelation, we see Jesus anxious to be with us in a personal friendship:

Listen! I am standing at the door, knocking; if you hear my voice and open the door, I will come in to you and eat with you, and you with me.

REVELATION 3:20

Jesus is always looking to develop a companionship with us. He wants us to open up and actually share our problems with Him. But He will never push His way into our lives, He only offers to come in and help. He simply knocks on our door and gives us the opportunity to accept His offer or reject it. But it's this close and personal relationship that is critical to our salvation. In order to move from being make-believers to true believers, we must walk closely with Him as friends naturally do. There is no other way.

But for some reason, we as Catholics generally have come to believe that our relationship with God does not need a personal element to such a degree. Somewhere along the line we got the impression that by going to Mass and frequenting the Sacraments, we should be all set for an automatic entrance into heaven, even if it's by way of purgatory.

A personal knowledge and love of God is what it takes to get into heaven. We are made poor by the lack of that personal knowledge and friendship with Jesus. As stated earlier, the poor Catholic is primarily someone who is hurting in some way or missing something very important in his or her life and this prevents them from walking closely with God. What they often don't realize is that they are hurt deep inside and what they need most can only be provided by Christ Himself. As long as they fail to seek Him out, their condition will only worsen. Going through all the outward motions of being a good Catholic will not cover up our true feelings about God and other people. He can see through our actions. He knows what's in the heart of man. If we never come to truly know and love Him, we will be lost.

But how can we tell if we truly do know Him? Is there a gauge or an indicator? Yes there is, as the first epistle of Saint John says:

> *Now by this we may be sure that we know him, if we obey his commandments. Whoever says, "I have come to know him," but does not obey his commandments, is a liar, and in such a person the truth does not exist; but whoever obeys his word, truly in this person the love of God has reached perfection. By this we may be sure that we are in him: whoever says, "I abide in him," ought to walk just as he walked.*
>
> 1 JOHN 2:3-6

Just because we were baptized Catholic, made our first communion and confirmation and so forth does not mean we know God. To gain heaven, we must keep His Commandments and we must have a personal knowledge and love of Him. However, going to church, frequenting the Sacraments, raising your children as Catholics and so forth are activities that people who do know God take part in. My point here is a fine one. Whatever truth rests in your heart will, in time, rise to the surface in your actions, for all to see. Your actions therefore do serve as proof or at least a good indicator of what is truly in your heart.

When you know Christ and love Him, it becomes obvious to everyone around you whether you are involved in church or any other religious routine or not. You'll always be looking for ways to help others. That's a telling characteristic of real Christians. They love people just as Jesus demonstrated a deep love for all those He came across. Furthermore, if we believe in Him, then He will save us and reward us with eternal life.

...because if you confess with your lips that Jesus is Lord and believe in your heart that God raised him from the dead, you will be saved.

ROMANS 10:9

Very truly, I tell you, anyone who hears my word and believes him who sent me has eternal life, and does not come under judgment, but has passed from death to life.

JOHN 5:24

Knowing God is the first key to gaining eternal life. It's the foundation upon which we build up our faith. Spend your time getting to know Him. Open that door when you hear Him knocking and He will come in and dine with you and you with Him.

2

The Early Years: Growing Up as a Catholic

Some of my earliest memories were of growing up on Long Island, New York, and of the nuns who were my teachers. Passionate and strict, they really appeared to believe what they taught us. Much of the curriculum revolved around memorization. We had to commit to memory certain parts of our first grade catechism and answer questions like "Who made you?" and "Why did God make you?" Perhaps my memories of these times are so strong not only because of the difficulty of the work but also because of the commitment of these women. They literally dedicated their lives to God. It had a real impact on me, even as a child.

Another strong memory was of my mother bringing me to first grade. After walking up what seemed to be a very long flight of stairs outside the school, we were greeted by a very stern looking nun. My mother let go of my hand, and at that point my teacher guided me into the building. It was cold and dreary looking and my desk was old and well used.

But the nuns' strict, hard exteriors did have soft spots. I remember waiting in the hall during my mother's parent/teacher meetings and being shocked to actually hear the nun laugh. "So, they are real people after all," I thought. For the most part, the nuns really did care for the children. It was hard for us children to see this because of their stringent discipline and demand for order in the classroom. We learned that God gave us strict rules so we could follow them and not get into trouble—and when we strayed from those rules in any direction, there would be a price to pay. In those days, corporal punishment was frequent. But what amazed many of us was that those who "got it" were usually the same ones that received the correction day in and day out. They seemed to enjoy the attention.

This caused me to wonder why the clergy were so strict with us. This was the late fifties and early sixties. They knew what we were going to encounter after graduation. The old order and ways of doing things were going away. So they tried to instill in us a spiritual conscience that could "save us" and protect us against the temptations we would soon encounter.

We often read Scripture in class and heard it in the Mass. But for some reason, we never read it directly from the Bible. Verses from Scripture were given to us in one or two sentences. Our teachers would always write the verses on the blackboard and we then would copy them into our daybooks. They wanted us to study these verses and to specifically take note of them as God's instructions to us, but it seemed we were not to ask too many questions beyond that point. The feeling we had was that the words of the Bible were themselves sacred and had to be handled with special care only by the priests and nuns. No one ever thought to actually study the Bible itself.

So while the process of learning about God did include the study of His Word and how He operated, not much attention was given to explaining why He wanted us to do certain things. We were told to just learn the verses, accept all the demands, and be obedient.

The focal point of our religious upbringing as Catholics was always the Mass. If anything was reinforced on a daily basis, it was the importance of going to Confession, Mass, and Holy Communion. Everything we were taught about God was centered in the Church itself—actually in the Tabernacle where God lived (as it seemed to us). We approached Church as a very important and special time. We always needed to be on our best behavior in God's house. We knew He could see us wherever we went and that He knew all about our activities both good and bad.

But still, there was a significantly sacred difference about the church experience. Church was unlike any other place we knew—it was literally holy ground, the place where God was really present. So it carried a special meaning and feeling for us. This specialness became even more pronounced when incense, special music and singing filled the air during Mass. I remember certain Mass celebrations in my childhood during which we could feel the presence of God in our lives the most. These impressions all worked together to create a certain level of devotion that, once experienced, the nuns and priests wanted us to nurture.

Recently, a friend was complaining to me about on how difficult it was to get her husband to Mass on Sundays. She said, "You know, I got him there last Sunday and the priest gave us a great talk on the Passion of Christ. But later on when I asked him about what he thought of the priest's homily, he admitted that he really wasn't listening. He was thinking about all the work he wanted to do around the house later that day." She let out a big sigh and then said, "Well, at least he was sitting in the Church at Mass and went to Communion." Her story brought back memories of a similar situation in my own family.

During my teen years, we would go to Mass every Sunday at a church conveniently located near our home. The 8:00 a.m. Mass fit my parents' schedule nicely, so it became part of our Sunday mornings. But the church was Polish in its origins and the entire Mass, including the Homily, was in Polish—a language none of us understood in my family. But my mother would always say, “As long as we go and are in His house, God knows and appreciates the effort.”

As incredible as this story may seem, it actually made some sense to us back then since we were accustomed to hearing the Mass celebrated largely in Latin. Vatican II had not yet had any real impact on Catholic Church life. There was always a fair amount of mystery surrounding the Mass—mystery that we, as Catholics, just accepted as something we would never understand. As long as the priest, our representative before God, knew what he was doing, we felt secure sitting in our pews. He was where he needed to be and we were where we needed to be. So going to a church that spoke Polish instead of Latin didn’t seem too ridiculous. Looking back, it’s very sobering to realize just how wrong we were in our understanding of God. Most frightening is that we all thought there was nothing wrong with what we were doing. We felt that God would approve of our intentions and at least give us credit for the effort. In hindsight, this was a great personal lesson, one that would significantly affect my future thinking.

Interestingly, I believe this mindset still exists today. Many Catholics see attendance at Mass as pretty much the sum total of their “duty” as Catholics. We think that as long as we go to Church, support it financially and treat everyone around us pretty decently, then God should be pretty happy with us. Unfortunately, too many of our spiritual teachers have settled for just encouraging us to go to church rather than develop a walking faith with Christ. Getting on to a personal level with God was a choice that seemed to be reserved for people who wanted to become members of a religious order—priests, nuns or brothers. But can you imagine saying that some of us need to be closer to God than others? Certainly every one of us has our calling and job in life, but we should each have a close, personal, and meaningful relationship with God.

During my high school years with the Franciscan Brothers, I for a time considered becoming a Priest or a Brother. There was some part of me that wanted a deeper relationship with God. But the only real option available to a Catholic who felt this way was to join the clergy. As Catholics, we never considered that we didn't have to become members of a religious order to be close to God, but as lay people could instead develop a personal, one-on-one walking faith with Him. This was not a well known concept and was never actively taught.

We heard homilies at Mass that told us we were to follow Christ, but it seemed that very few people in the congregation ever took that suggestion personally. Our only role models were the clergy members themselves. But somehow, we never considered them part of the real world. While we did see them most every day at school, they would rarely be seen downtown shopping or in other public places.

And of course as Catholic school children we had our uniforms, which we had to wear every day. Waiting every morning for the school bus, we would line up next to the children that were attending the local public school. They rode on one bus while we rode on another. We were different from them because of those uniforms and we knew it. We didn't know exactly what the difference was, but we knew it had something to do with God.

Isn't it interesting? We were identified as Catholics not necessarily because of our belief in God but because of our appearance. But for me, that was okay. Somehow, I felt that we had the better deal in going to a school where God was present and the teachers were strict. It was like having to eat spinach or broccoli every day. Even though I hated the taste, I knew that in the long run it would be healthier for me. Still, we did secretly wonder at times what it would be like not having to wear uniforms and be subject to such strict rules every day.

Prayer was another special experience for us. It occurred usually as a group activity during Mass or at other times such as when the Rosary was being said aloud. We were told to pray to God often, especially in the morning and at night before retiring for the day. But even at the tender age of five, the impression given to me was that God was very big and busy. We were told to "bother God" with our requests only when it was really necessary and this became a real issue for me. It made me feel as though God was too busy to be personally concerned about me.

No one ever said it to us directly, but we got the notion that if we were to access the Saints and Mary with our smaller and more frequent requests, they could intercede for us. This would keep our requests of God to an absolute minimum, thereby solving the problem. They, as it appeared to us, had more time on their hands than God or Jesus, and were therefore more able to hear our needs. They also seemed to know the best time to "catch" God and present these needs. They had the inside track, so to speak.

Repetition was also very critical during our prayer time in Church. It seemed that it was more important to pray the words of a standard prayer like the Our Father or Hail Mary over and over again rather than focus on the quality of the prayer. The protection and help we wanted from God appeared to come more from just saying the prayers repetitively, rather than focusing on understanding what the words meant and knowing who we were petitioning.

In the sixth grade, I had an embarrassing personal experience with the use of prayer for a specific purpose. A nun came up to me one day and told me to say three Hail Mary's every day for the protection of Mary. I took this to mean that for some reason Mary, the mother of God, was in need of protection. So, I prayed for her protection every day (for a very long time), until it dawned on me that it was me, not Mary, who needed the protection! Talk about blind obedience! Now, as silly as this story is, I believe that God still honored those prayers. But again it demonstrates the mechanical and rote manner of praying we were taught.

Overall, we were taught that God could be reached through prayer for our regular needs as well as our special requests. But in all cases we had to follow a certain protocol. Our prayers needed to be well organized and thought out. They had to be brief, to the point and timely. Panic or "911" type prayers were not encouraged; if we were truly staying close to God, such sudden, drastic pleas shouldn't be necessary.

But most of all, obedience in prayer was supremely important. We were to be like the Saints whose lives we studied in class. They possessed the ability to persevere in suffering through their prayers. The message was clear; real prayer was real work—but done properly, it could yield real positive results. I would not advocate teaching prayer this way to young people today. But in my case these habits ended up helping me stay close to God, even if I was not always personally aware of His presence.

Many of my friends and people I knew from my school days eventually left the Church and perhaps even God Himself. In their case, this method of teaching did not seem to work to their benefit. It is interesting. As many of these habits still remain with me today, I now see them in an entirely different light. Before, I would just repeat my prayers mechanically over and over. Now since I have developed a personal bond with God, these numerous prayers are part of our dialogue. The repetition has real meaning because of the real love in our relationship while before there was only a sense of duty and fear. What a difference!

Looking back on these experiences it's easy to see the strangeness of some of the things we did as children in Catholic school. But now, we have for comparison the experiences of our own children in public schools and religious education classes. There is clearly a tremendous difference. Because we are "more enlightened" today, young Catholics growing up do not always receive religious education from teachers possessing a strong passionate conviction of faith. It seems that the current thinking of many Catholics is to just try to be a good person and it is thought that this is an adequate position from which to teach religious concepts. As Jesus was a lot more than just a "good person" and since He should always be our model in all we try to do, we too have to strive to be more than just good people.

Additionally, it seems that many of the teaching materials used in religious education classes today have moved away from promoting the core principles of our Catholic faith. The current emphasis seems to be more on social justice type issues and being a good volunteer in our communities. To be sure, these are important concepts but should not replace learning the fundamental principles of our faith. Even more importantly, while it is possible to transmit knowledge to others in the form of information, it is literally impossible to transfer personal knowledge of God to another person unless he or she has actually come to know Him in a close intimate way. There is a great difference between knowing *of* someone as opposed to knowing him or her on a personal level. That's why our children must be encouraged to come to know Christ personally. Without this kind of familiarity with God, the real core of His principles cannot and do not "stick" for our young people. Learning about God in this kind of setting is like taking a history course; it's just for information purposes only. The facts will most likely be forgotten soon afterward.

So, the nuns would teach us the meaning of our prayers to the extent that we could understand but the emphasis once again, was on the activity of praying itself. Additionally, it seemed as if they just did not realize how some people like me were viewing our prayer time. When we were young, we came to understand that punishment was what happened when we did something wrong. The penalty was usually carried out in the form of a repetitive and boring task that made little or no sense at all. We understood that this was being done to us to perhaps make up for the wrong that we did. Unfortunately, prayer at times would fall into this category because it appeared to fulfill all the parts to the definition of punishment. Our teachers truly saw prayer as a way to maintain their own personal relationship with God and so naturally they pushed us to do the same. I believe they wanted for us the same kind of relationship they had with God. Why? Because many of them did have a personal bond with God. They were living it every day but sometimes just did not know how to express what they were experiencing. They knew it was something good and that we should be taught what they knew but they had difficulty in transferring that knowledge to us.

In many cases what they tried to teach us was oftentimes not understood and they became frustrated. But of course, we did not have that same level of rapport with God as they did. So the prayer exercises were often interpreted as something negative. They felt like punishment. This feeling was also reinforced in the Sacrament of Confession. Our penance was usually to be performed by saying the Our Father and Hail Mary many times over. The greater our sins, the more times we had to say these prayers. So many of us came to learn that prayer was a chore or in some cases, a form of penance. It was not seen as a way to enjoy fellowship with God or Jesus.

Confirmation was another moment in my Catholic upbringing that did not make a great deal of sense to me. It was presented to us as an event that marked our coming of age as Catholics. There was a great deal of mystery surrounding Confirmation. Something or someone called the Holy Ghost was to visit us on the occasion of the ceremony and with a small slap on the cheek by the Bishop, we were then to be considered real Catholics. This raised the whole question of who the Holy Ghost was in church life.

No matter how it was explained, it seemed that no one had a good understanding of this third person of the Trinity. He indeed was a ghost in that He moved quietly and invisibly about. Nonetheless, all of this mystery helped make my Confirmation experience vivid in my memory, so vivid that even to this day I can still remember certain parts of the ceremony. While preparing for the event, we learned new songs to sing in Church. One in particular, a song about becoming a soldier in Christ's army, still stands out in my mind. For the first time in my development as a Catholic, I began to get a real sense of being at risk because I was a Catholic. My friends and I all knew that soldiers could very easily lose their lives fighting for their country and I remember talking amongst ourselves about what it really meant to be confirmed. The whole conversation didn't make us feel good, but we once again we went along with the process and questioned little.

As young Catholics, the area of sin and confession also disturbed us greatly as it loomed constantly over our heads. Our teachers in grammar school and high school all felt that our spiritual health would be threatened most by our tendency to sin, so they put a great deal of effort into teaching us the details about sin. As children, we struggled greatly with the concept of sin as found in the Catholic faith. It unfortunately also gave rise to the concept of "Catholic guilt," long a stigma on Catholics individually and as a group.

We were taught that there are basically two types of sin in the Catholic faith: mortal and venial. Confession is the formal way to repair or fix the sins we commit, and as far as the Catholic Church is concerned, this is the only acceptable way to officially correct the wrongs that sin creates. We learned at a very early age that mortal sin, because of its serious nature, would keep us out of heaven. Venial sin, on the other hand, was presented as a minor offense to God; confessing venial sins was recommended but not imperative. But it was something we had to do on a weekly or even more frequent basis. Confession forced me to consider the ways I had offended God each week and consequently kept me thinking about God much of the time. But were my offenses mortal sins or not? That became the big question.

As I prepared for Confession, I went through a regular process of rationalization whereby any potential mortal sin could effectively be downgraded to the status of venial sin. It would be very embarrassing to admit to a priest that my activities during the week were that bad. All of my teachers knew me as a "good kid" in school and our parish priests knew many of us personally. We would see these priests during the week at school and we always felt that now, after Confession, they knew our darkest secrets. Even though the sins we're talking about here are mild by today's standards, at the time they seemed serious to us (it's another interesting way to gauge how far we, as a culture, have strayed down the wrong road). So for me, by downgrading the severity of the sins, I might even conclude that I did not have to tell the priest about them at all. For this very reason, on more than one occasion I can remember coming to the conclusion that Confession itself was not necessary that particular week. In the end, it was quite a game that I played. But others also played the game. I can remember a good friend of mine confiding in me saying that when he felt the urge to sin, he would make sure that he committed only a venial sin and not a mortal one. "If you have to sin," he would say, "make sure it's only a venial one, that way it can't hurt you that much." In a similar manner, many of us thought it best to keep a very low profile before God. For example, we would always sit in the back of the church—as if

God would be less likely to notice us there. This is still a common phenomenon in many churches today. The front pews are usually the last to fill up.

Our greatest fear in growing up was that we would get caught in a horrible trap: having just committed a mortal sin, we would die before we could confess it and be condemned to hell forever. One of the luckiest people ever presented to us in religion class was the thief on the cross who, just before he died, asked Jesus to let him into heaven. Jesus, as we know, did. We thought that was "very cool" and marveled at how fortunate he was since he obviously did something really bad to deserve crucifixion. He was probably headed to hell, we thought, when he met Jesus just at the last moment. How lucky can you be?

There was one other big question regarding sin, one that reveals much about our state of mind as young Catholics. We would wonder how much sin a person could absorb and still get into heaven. The concept of venial sin created an expectation that if a person continued to pile them up, they would at some point all add up to one big mortal sin. So we wondered where the breaking point was located.

Then there was the idea of the afterlife. Besides heaven and hell, there was the possibility of purgatory, where only Catholics could go when they died. On the surface it didn't sound like a place where you would want to go once you passed on from this life. But when compared to the alternative of hell, it seemed like a real bargain. After all, once you "did your time" in purgatory, you could enter heaven. It followed that if a person made purgatory their target to begin with, that meant they could ease up a bit in their efforts to remain sinless while on earth.

It didn't take me long to realize that trying to remain absolutely pure and chaste every day was next to impossible. So purgatory, not heaven, became the goal for me and many others. Even many of our teachers talked openly on this topic and agreed with us. We knew that we would never be good enough to make it to heaven directly after we died, so we resigned ourselves to accepting the next best thing.

I remember feeling as if a great weight had been taken off of my shoulders once I adopted this attitude and focus. I could relax more and not be so paranoid about committing mortal sins. After all, life was hard enough. Now going through each day with all of its temptations was like working a high wire act with purgatory as the net and hell being the hard ground below. "Thank God for the net!" I would think.

Right about now, most of you reading this are probably just shaking your heads and saying something like, "Wow, this poor guy was really way off, wasn't he?" And you would be right in your assessment. The fact is that I *was* way off and it would not be until my forty-first birthday that God would come back into my life and show me how far I had drifted from Him and the truth about Him.

My move away from God happened gradually over a number of years. The "drift" away from our Lord was imperceptible and very subtle in nature. I was not directly aware of the growing distance between God and myself. It wasn't until I started to feel very unhappy and discontented with my daily work and life routine that I began to think about what had changed in my life.

Thinking back to that critical midpoint of my life, it is a constant source of personal amazement for me to realize how God can work with people and retrieve them from the various places they've gone in their thinking and behavior. He can and will do this as long as we allow Him to come into our life which is a critical point. He always needs out personal permission to renovate and restore any broken part of our life.

Seeing opinion polls on current issues, reading Christian polling data and working with many clients over the years has convinced me that many Catholics have maintained a system of beliefs—let's call them "make-beliefs"—similar to the ones I've described. Our actions do speak louder than our words. We actively pursue the things we want and customize our beliefs to justify those pursuits. We are very good at deceiving ourselves and rationalizing our behavior when something we want badly is at stake. For a long time my own behavior fit this description as well. And even as I write these words, I know that there are certain areas of sin in my life which still exist and that need to be dealt with soon.

The truth is that we have become comfortable in our sin. Many of us have constructed a belief system that will allow us to keep and cherish certain sinful desires while giving God what we think He wants from us, up to a certain point. That belief system is basically the same one that formed in us when we were children. But even though many of us have gotten older and wiser, our system of beliefs has apparently matured very little. However, many of us have modified it so that it will allow us to have the things we want whether they are good for us or not. In a sense, we have found a way to disconnect the moral alarm system (our conscience) which is an integral part of our beliefs and core values. This is what we rely on to alert us when we're about to get involved in something wrong. Let me illustrate. A few years ago, a friend of mine quite unexpectedly began to share with me how he relates with God. He said:

"You know, one day a long time ago, me and God had to come to an understanding, because things between us were not good. After we sat and 'talked,' we came to an agreement where He got something of what He wanted and I got what I wanted. He knew I was weak in certain areas and could never perform to the level He expected, so He agreed to accept me just as I was, sin and all. And I realized that I had to give in on certain things He wanted, so I picked the ones that I felt I could reasonably accomplish.

Do I believe in God? Sure, yes, of course I do!
Is He my Lord and Savior? He certainly is!
Do I feel born again? Sure, yes, of course I am!"

Not a bad deal, is it? But what did my friend do? He accepted Christ as his Lord and Savior not on God's terms, *but on his own terms,* according to his own needs. I remember walking away from that conversation thinking about how wrong-headed this guy was in his beliefs. I even remember (God forgive me), laughing out loud on the way home as to how wrong he was, until God convicted *me*. When I thought about it, I was guilty of doing the same thing in my own life. I was cutting my own deal with God in a number of life areas, and that's not how it is supposed to work. Similarly, I don't say to my wife, "Listen honey, you know I've got a real weakness for other women, something I really can't control. So just once in a while I need to go off on a 'toot.' You understand, don't you? But when I come back, I'll be good and I'll take care of whatever you want done around the house."

This is not how God wants or expects us to treat those we love, including Him. If I truly love my wife, I honor our marriage vows, all the time. If I truly love God, then I honor that relationship as well by doing the things He wants and not doing the things that will hurt Him and His love for me.

In my case, it would have been so easy to blame my state of mind on my upbringing as a Catholic, especially since my experience was obviously lacking something important. But I would gain nothing by blaming my teachers or the Catholic Church itself for my spiritual ignorance. I still am, in part at least, a make-believer and the power to change that always rests within me. It's a battle that goes on every day in my life.

From an overall point of view, the clergy taught us well in my early years. No, they did not teach us directly about developing a close, personal walk with the Lord. But they implied it and more importantly, *modeled* it for us, to the best of their abilities. We have to remember, very few people were openly honest about what they believed concerning God in those days. We rarely saw anyone practicing their faith in public, with the exception of members of religious orders. So the only role models we had were our teachers at school. We can criticize the Catholic clergy all we want but let's face it: Who else was even attempting to live the kind of model life that God expects of us? They pointed each one of us in a direction that eventually could bring us to a place where we would have a chance of getting close to God.

Most importantly, they kept God in front of us throughout our formative years. It was their efforts that accustomed us to having God around us, so when it was time for the "prodigal son or daughter" to come home, we would know where to go. Their methods may be open to criticism but for me personally, the result turned out to be vitally important.

So in the end, the same all-important bottom line that drives God in His dealings with us, also drove the people who taught us about God. If we stand back and review the effort of people such as those who taught us about God in our formative years, it's very difficult to ignore the amount of sheer devotion, passion, conviction and love it must have taken. But why would people do this? What makes the clergy and lay clergy work so hard to spread the truth about Christ? The answer is simple: *They believe that God is real and that He exists as you and I do here and now.* They also believe that God's ultimate goal is to bring all of His children back home to be with Him. Since that is His highest goal then it becomes their chief pursuit as well.

As I mentioned already, after everything is said and done in this life, all the money made and spent, all the diseases treated, all the divorces, hatred, and happy times are experienced, there is only one thing that matters in the end. We need to be on the inside of the gates to heaven at the end of that last day.

What else could be more important? It was so important to God, the maker of the universe, that He chose to send His only Son to take on our sins and die for us so that we could gain heaven (see John 3:16). All of His efforts are designed to get us home in the end, as this is His greatest desire. See how Saint Peter explained it in his last words before he died:

The Lord is not slow about his promise, as some think of slowness, but is patient with you, not wanting any to perish, but all to come to repentance. But the day of the Lord will come like a thief, and then the heavens will pass away with a loud noise, and the elements will be dissolved with fire, and the earth and everything that is done on it will be disclosed.

2 PETER 3:9-10

Peter promises that God will do everything He can to get us home with Him—but he also warns that, in time, the doors to heaven will close. All of my teachers throughout my religious education knew this very same thing and believed it. To a certain extent it drove them to work even harder at explaining the truth about God. Just consider it: God creates a world that He knows will be flawed to such an extent that He will ultimately need to offer His Son as an atonement, in the most gruesome and terrible form of death known to man. He will agree to do this so that we, His children, will again have the opportunity to get into heaven. Of all the stories I have ever heard in my life, this story of Christianity is the most insane. But what is even more insane is that we as Catholics, believe it! Couldn't God have found another way to accomplish His goals? Couldn't God have just started all over again after Adam and Eve failed Him? Why go through the terrible pain of having His Son die for us? Theologians will try to explain this with complicated terms and theories. But no one really knows why except to say that because of His great love for us, He did it.

Ultimately, we can only theorize about this, which tells us that because of its importance, this is not something to be guessing at or speculating about. It's enough for us to know that God chose to do this. Since He did, then there must be something incredibly terrible and horrible waiting for us in the next life if He didn't take this action to save us. The Passion and Death of Jesus Christ cost God an incredible amount, a cost we are incapable of conceiving. So trying to understand it fully is a waste of time. If we truly believe in God, we simply need to accept Him as being true and just comply with God's instructions. And we need to understand that on the last day, God will *not* be saying something like, "Oh well, I guess it's okay, everyone can enter heaven regardless of what they said, did and believed on earth."

More than we can imagine is hanging in the balance right now. The price was too high, the stakes too great and even though the level of His love is extremely high, God is still a *just* God. He will demand that justice be done on that last day because just as love is in His nature, it is also in His nature to seek and deal out fairness. Consider His explanation to the Pharisees in the following verses:

> *Woe to you, scribes and Pharisees, hypocrites! For you tithe mint, dill, and cummin, and have neglected the weightier matters of the law: justice and mercy and faith. It is these you ought to have practiced without neglecting the others. You blind guides! You strain out a gnat but swallow a camel!*
>
> MATTHEW 23:23-24

The Pharisees didn't care about being just, fair and compassionate—but according to Jesus, justice was so important that it could cost them everything in the end.

I believe God's sacrifice of his Son gives us insights into a different side of Him. This sacrificial aspect of God is also part of His nature. The sacrifice of His Son was in payment for all of our sins, from Adam down to all people. He did it to give us all a good chance at avoiding the horror of hell. Christ's action on the cross took the whole human race "off of death row." Without it, none of us would ever have a chance of gaining heaven. Quite literally, His action saved us. This is where His mercy and love enter the picture for us. It is up to us to accept Christ as lovingly offered by God on the cross, so we can be set free from the power of death.

There is therefore now no condemnation for those who are in Christ Jesus. For the law of the Spirit of life in Christ Jesus has set you free from the law of sin and of death.

ROMANS 8:1-2

This is who we encounter every day in our lives: the Holy Spirit, as He works under the new law, the law of the spirit, instituted by Christ in the New Testament.

The bottom line is that we need to get very serious about our relationship with God. We cannot know all the answers before we choose to serve Him, or even as we serve Him. So the answer to the impossible sounding questions such as why God would create a race of people that He knew would fail Him is simple: because He loves us. And because we love Him, we do what He asks of us, while we still have the time. Listen carefully to His instructions and follow them. As I heard a minister once say, "We all need eyeglasses for our ears. We need to hear Him correctly. Our eternal lives depend on it."

All of these thoughts and experiences, from my youth in first grade up into adulthood, formed the foundation for my faith. But for a long time, I lived with just the foundation and nothing more. Even though I thought I had a "faith structure," in reality

I had nothing. I was a make-believer and as such I had built nothing significant on that foundation. I was too busy making money, raising a family, and attending to my own things. But that was all about to change.

3

Life Before *In His Steps*

After eighteen years of solid Catholic education, I had stopped maturing spiritually. At forty-one years of age, I had the religious convictions of a teenager! It's not even accurate to call them convictions because they would change with whatever situation confronted me. They were adaptable to my needs of the moment, assuming that I even bothered to think of them at the time. My attendance at church was infrequent at best. Whether or not I went to Confession, I went to Holy Communion automatically and without thought.

Matters of faith and religion were mostly extraneous and useless in my real world of everyday living, especially with regard to business issues. God was to be kept handy only for the emergency calls. Much of my spiritual activity was simply robotic and rote. I considered Mass boring and the priest's homily, including the readings from Scripture, a mere matter of formality. The words would just bounce off of me. At that time, the *rhythm* of the Mass remained more in my memory than anything else. Even my prayers were lifeless and had a quantitative rather than qualitative air to them. In short, I had become a *mechanical Catholic.*

It was strictly out of a sense of duty and obligation that I remained in my Catholic faith. Many of my friends had stopped practicing their faith or moved on to other religions. I continued to attend Church and had something of a relationship with God, but it was sorely lacking the kind of life He wanted to see. You might say that my faith had gone into a coma—and no one ever knows what condition comatose patients will be in if and when they ever come out of it. My relationship with God was distant at best. I was still convinced that He was too busy to hear me on a regular basis and so my conversation with Him was mechanical and sterile. And since I didn't know God as a friend, I could not talk to Him as one. My obedience to Him (if you could call it that) was based on fear and a sense of obligation, rather than on love.

Like a light switch, I would turn Him on only when I felt I needed help in seeing important things more clearly. And I feared that if "His light" was left on too long, He would start to point out those dark corners in my life where things were dirty, unorganized and that needed attention badly. So it wasn't often that I invited God into my life for advice or help. I usually felt that I could handle most everything myself just fine. Besides, my work and business were the center of my life at this time. Even though most of our clients were decent and fairly predictable, I always had my suspicions about people. "Watch out for that one" informed many of my relationships with clients and acquaintances. I tried not to be a businessperson who was known as a "bad guy" but I would do anything considered marginally ethical by worldly standards to protect my family and business interests. There were times when we, as a firm, could afford to be compassionate toward others but those occasions were not very frequent. If people didn't pay us for some reason, small claims court or a collection agency was an automatic response.

I even felt that our employees, to whom we gave many benefits, were taking advantage of my good nature. I remember one particular occasion when my frustration with certain employees reached such a level that I installed a punch clock that very same day. Because one or two people who were not being honest with their hours, I over-reacted and penalized everyone when I should have dealt directly with those people. Instead I declared war on my entire staff. It showed me how generally disgusted I had become with my work. Actually, this event became the "straw that broke the camel's back." But then came April 19, 1990, a date that changed everything for me.

A Little Book that Asks "What Would Jesus Do?"

Many of us can point to a special moment in time when our lives changed in a most important way. Perhaps it was a change in life direction, or the awakening of feelings about someone or something special. The changes would be strong enough to alter the course we followed from that point forward. For me, this happened about fourteen years ago.

It was just after our tax season, early in 1990. My wife and I decided to get away with our children and take a trip to Lancaster County in Pennsylvania. My frame of mind was not healthy to begin with because of our experience with that year's tax season at the office. Many of our clients seemed dissatisfied with the results of their tax returns. Some expected greater refunds than they were getting and others, expecting refunds, ended up owing the Internal Revenue Service. In addition, the economy in our state had slipped into a major recession. As accountants, we took the brunt of our clients' unhappiness. On top of this, I was tired. It was that kind of exhaustion that comes from doing something over and over to the point where it becomes very difficult to see any long-term benefits or purpose to the work. To make matters worse, my children were not too eager to sit in a car for a 6-hour drive and they let me know it, frequently throughout the trip.

I'll remember the date—April 19, 1990—for as long as I live.

We arrived in time for dinner at our hotel and afterward we visited a small nearby strip mall looking for souvenirs. Just about every store in the mall was closed and I remember standing outside of the pharmacy waiting for my family and feeling very discouraged and discontented. At the end of the mall I saw a small Christian bookshop. It looked closed, but I found myself wandering over toward it and discovered that it was open.

Now, Christian bookstores were not one of my favorite places to visit. As a matter of fact, I had never been in one before that day; I had no reason to. I entered and an elderly man came out of the back portion of the store and said hello. At that moment, a paperback book on a nearby bottom shelf caught my eye. Its cover had a beautiful picture of trees and fields in an autumn setting. Picking it off the shelf, I heard him say, "Oh, you'll like that one." It was entitled *In His Steps* by Charles Sheldon. The cover boasted "30,000,000 copies sold." This caused me to wonder what book, other than the Bible, would sell so many copies. It intrigued me, so I bought it, took it back to our hotel room and began to read.

The book told a story about the members of a particular church who were being faced with an interesting and challenging dilemma. They were all wondering what it truly meant to be a Christian, or for that matter, followers of Jesus Christ. They were known in their town as a comfortable and well-to-do church, but lacking in spiritual commitment. Their discussion about the question moves the congregation to take action. They all take an oath, swearing that for a period of one year they would not make any decision without first asking the question, "What would Jesus do?" They pledged to follow whatever they thought the answer to that question was in their own personal situation.

As you can imagine, this ends up changing each of their lives and the lives of the people around them. I found the proposition intriguing. Nothing like this had ever presented itself to me in all of my business experience or spiritual upbringing. What made it even more interesting was that many of the characters in the story were businesspeople like me. I wondered, "Would it be possible to actually do something like this in today's business world? Could Jesus really play a major role in how we deal with one another every day, especially in a business setting where money is involved?"

It seemed too idealistic and naive, but I found myself wishing out loud that this proposition could be true. At that point in my life, I needed to know that there was a better way to work at my job. I realized later on that *In His Steps* was the vehicle that God used to get me started on my way back home to Him. It's particularly important to note how He worked in this event. He chose to use something that He knew would get my attention at this particular moment in my life. Also, He arranged circumstances so as to maximize the probability that I would respond positively to His call. It is amazing how He works. At the time, it wasn't obvious to me as to what changes were to take place. But, this little book was about to help me find the answers to my questions and change my life, as it had done to millions who had read it before me.

PART II

TIME SPENT WITH GOD

4

Life After *In His Steps*

A very special moment occurred right after I had finished reading *In His Steps.* While driving to an appointment one day, a strong feeling came over me, an insight that dawned gradually in my mind. God seemed to be saying to me, "So, you asked me for a wonderful wife, didn't you? You also wanted two beautiful children and a pretty house in the country with a long driveway? And didn't you ask me for a profitable accounting practice in a small country town and a strong sense of success and accomplishment? Well, I gave you all of these things, didn't I? Now I need something in return from you."

It suddenly dawned on me that God was not too big or busy to be involved with me on a personal level. There were no bells, whistles or fireworks. It was just a quiet and peaceful sense that I was in His presence. I also realized then that a relationship with God is like a friendship with someone that means a great deal to you. When they need you, it doesn't even cross your mind that it might be inconvenient for you to respond to their needs then and there. You just drop everything and go. It's like that with our Lord, as well it should be! After all, you are on his Road to Grace and as you move closer and closer to Him, He responds in more frequent and intimate ways. Expect it—it can easily happen this way.

But it's been very difficult to explain to people just how suddenly things changed for me. Simply put, God became visible in a certain way. I could sense His reality and more importantly, became convinced of His presence. While I couldn't see Him directly as I would another person, there was too much evidence of His real presence in my life. There were too many coincidences and too much revelation to ignore. Something big had changed and I could feel it.

Even more amazing was the realization that He planned on working with me to accomplish what He had in mind. This knowledge paralyzed me for a while. All my years of believing just the opposite about God prevented me from moving forward in this new direction. I never thought in a million years that God would ever notice me, much less approach me to do something for Him. As I said earlier, my goal was always to maintain a low profile with God. But slowly the inertia left me and a strong desire to read His word in Scripture overtook me. Many of the verses I read were also found in the catechism of the Catholic Church. That was a pleasant surprise for me because I had always heard people criticize the Catholic Church for not adhering to Scripture as much as it should. With help from a book of commentary that explained Scripture passages, my eyes began to open. Finally, after forty-one years, the marvelous world of God's word revealed itself to me.

One day for example, someone was explaining the concept of the Trinity and how it works. He drew an analogy between the three persons of the Trinity and the sun. He said that God is like the sun, around which everything else revolves. Jesus is like the light we see coming from the sun, because He is the part of God that came to earth for all to see. The Holy Spirit is like the warmth and energy we feel coming directly from the sun. Taken all together you have one entity, one presence, producing three different effects on us.

It was a marvelously simple explanation and a real revelation to me. It made a difficult concept easier to comprehend. It demonstrated to me that as we move closer to God, He would reveal things to us that we didn't see clearly before. This filled me with hope and confidence and it confirmed my thoughts about being a poor Catholic and finding myself on the Road to Grace. This experience was in stark contrast to everything else in my life which seemed to have few or no clear answers. It provided me with fresh proof that I was on the right road, heading toward whatever God wanted me to accomplish.

Soon, Christ became more and more real to me, and I could no longer ignore or discount Him. Now I had a choice to make: Either make believe He did not exist or care about me or respond to Him personally. I chose the latter option.

When I did, it soon became obvious that God had always been near me from the very beginning. It was like the poem *Footprints*, in which the narrator thinks that God had abandoned him during the tough times of his life. As he and God look back over those times he sees only one set of footprints, not two. He assumes that they were his. Of course they weren't; they were Christ's, left from the times when Jesus carried him. This was my experience as well and the revelation was humbling. It certainly explained all the "near misses" I had as a young person.

God had obviously intervened the time when my car stayed on the road narrowly missing a tree it could have easily hit. He was with me on a water-skiing adventure when the boat's outboard motor got dangerously close to my legs—yet missed me, even as I felt the violent churning of the propeller as it went by. Then there were the life-threatening complications that accompanied the birth of my son and his fragile new life. But he survived and we survived. And the list goes on and on, when I think about it.

I now realize that this is how God works. The more we

respond to His invitations to become close, the more He intervenes in our lives in a good way. He doesn't necessarily prevent bad things from touching us, but He'll help us get through those tough times with His supernatural love and care. Remember, God does not necessarily airlift us out of the hole we find ourselves in from time to time. But He will support us as we climb out.

Another major revelation came from two particularly interesting pieces of Scripture concerning Satan, somebody no one likes to think about except in fantasies or movies. These passages describe our world as a place where Satan is real and very much present:

You were dead through the trespasses and sins in which you once lived, following the course of this world, following the ruler of the power of the air, the spirit that is now at work among those who are disobedient.

EPHESIANS 2:1-2

For our struggle is not against enemies of blood and flesh, but against the rulers, against the authorities, against the cosmic powers of this present darkness, against the spiritual forces of evil in the heavenly places.

EPHESIANS 6:12

Isn't it interesting? When Hollywood makes a horror film about the devil and the terror he creates, people will flock to the theatre to see it. But do we think the devil is real or not? I found it to be very logical that if there really is a God and Jesus is in the world, then what the Bible says about Satan must also be true. Why? Because Christ came down to earth to save us from something terrible, something like hell and Satan. What else could we need to be saved from? That simple fact is worth thinking about. This then led me to have another major thought. I found that we cannot pick and choose only the parts of the Bible we like or that make sense to us. The whole book is either true or false. There can be no middle ground—for if there is, how can we know (and who would decide) which parts are true and which aren't?

But what shocked me even more was when I realized that my job was to help God get all of His children—or at least those that lived, worked and socialized near me every day—back home, even though there is evil all around us. Actually this is the task assigned to each of us who come to know Him. God's ultimate desire is to see us home with Him forever in heaven (see John 6:39). On the other hand, Satan's ultimate purpose and desire is to populate hell—and all of us are his targets. Sobering isn't it? When we realize this fact, the people that we encounter in our workday lives are no longer just customers, co-workers, friends or family any more. Suddenly, the relationship I had with each person in my life took on an eternal meaning—and I wondered how many of them truly realized what was going on in the spiritual world around us. Everyone became a brother or sister who needed to see the truth about what's coming toward us in the future.

Here I learned a very important lesson about prayer. I could never hope to have a meaningful relationship with every person I come into contact with every day. So how could I tell them what I've been learning about God? I couldn't, plain and simple. But as I see these people every day, even at a ball game or concert, I can pray that each will hear from God sooner or later. I can ask God to send other people into their lives wherever they go. Of course if the opportunity presents itself, I can directly tell others about God as well.

And then, as if God wanted to reinforce this revelation, something else happened which still causes me to marvel at how

He works. It actually confirmed and clarified many things to me.

It was Christmas of 1990, that same year when *In His Steps* came into my life. My family was opening gifts when my wife pointed to a Christmas card on the back side of the Christmas tree. I frowned and commented that we never exchanged Christmas cards before and why start now. Well, she got up and handed it to me and said, "Please just open it, honey."

Marcia and I met twenty years earlier and somehow she knew that we were to be married. As usual, it took me a little bit longer to figure the same thing out for myself. The card she wrote spoke of how from the moment we met she knew we were meant for each other. She also knew in her heart that I was not "saved" as a Catholic Christian (Marcia came from a Protestant background. More about the term "saved" later on). So, she began to pray privately for me, that I would someday come to know Jesus Christ as my Lord and my Savior. Now that it had finally happened, she wanted to tell me just how happy she was that this occurred.

Reading her words in that Christmas card just melted me. And they taught me a valuable lesson: Never discount what we do for others in the privacy of our homes, cars or offices. It's not the publicity that counts; it's the closeness we achieve with Christ that produces the results we need. The power to change anything rests with God—and *He can change anything*. We just have to learn how to get close enough to Him through prayer to access His power and love. And He could not be any more receptive to this idea—He wants our love and friendship more than anything else. Finding Christ to be real, took a long time for me, but I'm convinced it happened simply because of someone else's prayer and love for God. Never, ever, underestimate the power of prayer. It is like a life-giving umbilical cord from God to us.

Another big change that occurred in me since reading *In His Steps* had to do with sin. Playing the old game of ignoring or downplaying the significance of my sins no longer became an option for me. My sin was not to be hidden from God, it was to be taken to God to be forgiven, as soon as possible, and my relationship with Him restored. Revelation struck again when I suddenly realized that all sin, not just mortal sin, was offensive to God. Venial sins lost their meaning to me. Any sin, serious or insignificant, was to be rooted out immediately and taken to God.

Paying attention to my personal behavior became more important. I needed now to examine everything before me and act from God's perspective on the choices I faced every day. That meant I needed to acquire the "mind of Christ," and it drove me back to the Scriptures to get a better understanding of God and how His mind works. My dealings with people started to change, newly informed by the question, "What would Jesus do?" It took me quite a while to adapt to this new way of thinking and it still is a struggle for me from time to time. Try asking yourself that question before making your next decision. It can be very revealing.

To illustrate how profoundly my relationship with God changed, think back to the time when you first fell in love with someone special. Whenever you could, you wanted to be with that person and would never think of doing anything to hurt them or upset them. If you did anything to offend them, you would rush to send flowers, say you're sorry and do whatever it took to repair the hurt. Similarly, I can no longer live comfortably if I know that I have hurt Him. The strange thing was that before *In His Steps,* it was not as if God was very far from me. It was just that I couldn't bring myself to develop a real friendship with Him on a personal level.

In a similar vein, many of my college friends and those who became acquaintances later on in life seemed to work very hard at trying to escape from God and the requirement of developing that personal link with Him. People ask me if I was "born again" after reading *In His Steps.* Here's what Jesus said about that:

Jesus answered him, "Very truly, I tell you, no one can see the kingdom of God without being born from above."

JOHN 3:3

Jesus was emphasizing how important it is to change our old ways and adopt new ones that are more in line with what God wants from us.

It's a phrase like "being saved" which indicates a person has acknowledged that God is the center of his or her life. And as it says in the catechism, we become members of God's people through this rebirthing process.

One becomes a member of this people not by a physical birth, but by being 'born anew,' a birth 'of water and the Spirit,' that is, by faith in Christ, and Baptism. (CCC 782)

Everything they do from that point forward needs to be in compliance with God's will. This implies that they must be in constant and accurate contact with Him in order to know what He wants of us. In short, Jesus needs to become our Lord as well as our Savior. I had long ago accepted Him as my Savior. But accepting Him as Lord is a whole different story and can be much more difficult to accomplish.

This word "Lord" means that a person will do whatever God asks of him or her. This idea caused me great difficulty and still does from time to time. It was like that pledge those people took in *In His Steps.* They agreed to do whatever Jesus would do in their place. That took great courage of conviction and belief in their God as their Lord. He controlled their lives. It also involved a yielding of their wills over to God's will. Giving up my will to

God sounded very drastic and difficult for me to do.

But think about the Lord's Prayer (or the Our Father, as some may call it). In it we pray, "thy kingdom come, thy will be done" and actually ask God to do His will for us in our lives. Why? Because when Jesus gave us this prayer to say (Matthew 6: 9-13), He knew that God knows what is best for us in all cases. Therefore He wanted us to always go to God and seek His will for our lives, so we wouldn't make the wrong choices.

But do you realize you're asking God to do this for you? When you say that prayer, you are saying, in essence, "Forget my will Lord, you know what's best for me, so let's do it your way." You can probably imagine how silly I felt after all those years of saying the Our Father and expecting to get things my way all the time.

But after forty-one years, I realized that God did answer my prayers after all. He gave me His will, which was the best thing for me in the end. But it took me a long time to realize this truth—so be careful of not only what you pray for but also how you pray!

This is another good example why we need to study the Scriptures in detail. It is very possible to misunderstand the words we are using in our own prayers. We may say them one way not realizing that we have asked God for something different than what we had in mind. This may explain why we do not understand His responses to our prayers sometimes because we simply have asked incorrectly.

So, you may wonder if after reading Sheldon's book had I been "born again"? This whole question balances on another question—did I now truly believe in Jesus Christ as my Lord and Savior? Without a doubt, the most famous piece of Scripture from the Bible is John 3:16 which states, *"For God so loved the world that he gave his only Son, so that everyone who believes in him may not perish but may have eternal life."*

The truth of this critical verse, rests on this one word, "believes." This verse is talking about each one of us as we make up our minds about Christ, and it is up to each one of us to come to a decision about that one word.

Let's look at the meaning of the word "believes" as it is used in John 3:16. I have found that there are three levels to the state of "believing". First, something can make sense to you intellectually, so you can accept it as fact.

The second level is believing as you do when you become passionate about something. We all know someone who can get really excited about a topic. They become fervently enthusiastic about what they are saying or involved with. Their belief goes deeper into the heart region and they feel beyond all doubt that their belief is true.

At the third level, you believe in something so ardently, so powerfully, that you can no longer eat, sleep, drink, etc., until you act on that belief. This level of belief is visceral—you feel and think so strongly about something that it changes how you act in front of other people, even in front of strangers in public.

This is what happened to me. Christ became so real that I had to do something about Him. I had to believe in Him on a personal level or I had to forget about Him. I simply came to believe in Christ as explained in John 3:16. If you want to call that being born again or being saved, that's fine. But please don't get the impression that believing was the hard part. My hard-driving nature and spirit of independence made making the commitment God demanded difficult, to say the least. But what made my commitment to Him almost impossible to sustain was that certain members of my family and people that knew me out in the business world, just could not understand that God wanted my belief in Him to extend to all areas of my life.

My poor father would say to me, "What is this religion thing about? You seem to be going overboard with it. Now listen to me. There is no place for this on the job. You go to work, do the best you can for your customers, take care of your family's needs and then, if you have extra time, you can do this religion thing as a hobby, maybe."

Early in 2001 Dad passed away and I don't know that he ever understood what I was feeling or hoped to accomplish. We talked about the Bible and how important it was for him to read it for himself, so he could make up his own mind. He agreed to try but he just could not make sense out of the words. Now, my father was a voracious reader. He had a library of the classics and loved books about history and politics. But still he could not make any sense of God's words in the Bible. He went to church most of his life, heard the words of the Bible spoken at Mass, but could not read or understand them for himself.

It was such a terrible feeling not being able to minister to my own Dad during his greatest hour of need. But again, I had to trust that God was in control of the situation and that He would take care of him. So I simply continued to pray for him, asking God to do whatever needed to be done so that my father would be in heaven someday.

Agreeing to take the first step toward becoming something of a disciple of Jesus Christ was a major event for me. Again, I was not aware of it then but at that time I was and still am in the process of losing my poorness as a Catholic. I was seeking God and the kind of gifts and lessons He wanted to teach me. I really look back on that time now as something incredible. I was lost... and He found me. He invited me to step onto the Road to Grace and I accepted. Life hasn't been the same since.

While it hasn't been easy, I have a curious comfort in knowing where I am headed. The challenges in my life have grown but now I have access to the ultimate form of help and aid: Jesus Christ.

So, today my walk with Christ takes place not just on weekends in church or at home with my family, but also at work with employees, co-workers, customers, competitors, people that like me and people that don't. It even gets into my social life. As a matter of fact, the real tests of my loyalty and commitment to God are even greater outside the home and the church setting. Why? Because outside of the home and church is where it is most likely that we will encounter people we don't like or who don't like us or agree with us. It is much harder to "love others" when they are being quite unlovable toward us.

This is especially true when dealing with business competitors, people that owe you money or a boss who's being very difficult with you. It is a daily challenge to work through these obstacles. The twelve Disciples had to work with similar challenges and they had Christ Himself physically looking over their shoulders with His expectations for each of them. Taking up the call of Christ to follow Him is the biggest challenge you'll ever face, but having the knowledge that you are trying to do what God wants of you is just simply an incredibly wonderful feeling. There is nothing else like it on the face of the earth.

5

Nice Story, But It's All Optional, Right?

It wouldn't surprise me if many of you are right now thinking something like:

"Nice story, but I don't think this walking faith thing is quite right for me. I'm happy for you, but it just sounds like it would be too difficult, restrictive and boring. So I would like to pass on this, can't I? I mean all this you're talking about is really optional, isn't it? You don't have to go through all of this to get into heaven, do you?"

This is the question that all Catholics must ultimately answer sooner or later. But before we can, we first need to realize how God works in this area. There are plenty of excuses for not getting closer to God. Some people may feel that they've lived a certain way for so long and cannot see the need to move any closer to God. Others may feel that they are too old to change and that getting more intimate with God would just be too disruptive and unsettling. Perhaps they just simply cannot picture themselves suddenly becoming so "holy." Or they are afraid of embarrassment.

But think about what's at stake and consider the alternative. What will happen if you don't follow Christ in all that you do? Is following Christ really an option or not?

In the Bible, Jesus talks about giving a knowledge of Himself to those who seek Him.

The following verse explains what will happen to those who are content not to grow in their relationship with God. I believe it relates directly to the question of whether following Christ is optional.

> *For to all those who have, more will be given, and they will have an abundance; but from those who have nothing, even what they have will be taken away.*
>
> MATTHEW 25:29

Jesus is telling us to use, to the best of our ability, whatever we are blessed with in life. However, this verse has to do mainly with our belief in God. Even a little bit of faith to start with can be enough to gain us more and more faith. It will continue to grow as long as we continue to look for Him and use what we have to the best of our abilities (see the Parable of the Talents in Matthew 25:14-30).

But if we allow "laziness of heart" to keep us from getting closer to God, then we can expect to lose even the little bit of understanding and relationship we already have with Him. In other words, use it or lose it! We're either growing in Christ or receding from Christ.

Do you remember what I said earlier about being a forty-one year-old with the faith understanding of a child? That's exactly what was happening to me. Because I was not looking to increase my knowledge and relationship with God, I was slowly losing that which I had built up over the years of Catholic instruction. The kind of life I was leading was eroding the effectiveness of my walk with God.

God says that if you make even a small attempt at learning about Him, He'll help you along in the process and eventually accomplish a great deal more. If you wish to go further with God, the simple answer is to just start looking for Him. He'll bring you into contact with others who are seeking Him too.

But most important of all is to start reading His Word. Get yourself a Bible with a modern day translation and a Bible commentary that will explain the verses you read. It's one thing to read the Scriptures and quite another to understand them. Remember, you are trying to get to that third level of belief and the only way to accomplish that is to allow God to grow your belief in Him. Then it will become a belief so powerful that it affects all of your actions and behavior.

So, is following Christ optional? Well, because we have free will, it is optional. You are not required to develop a close faith walk with God, but there is no other sure way to gain eternal life if you do not have that close walking faith with God. At some point we must make up our minds to either step out onto that Road to Grace or stay where it's comfortable… for now. But let's be very clear about this. For the people who are content to just sit back and do little or nothing to increase their closeness to God, they then will lose even the little bit of faith they had to begin with. Where then will that leave them?

The following verses from the New Testament are the words of Jesus Himself and appear more than once in the Bible. Read what Jesus said about a certain group of people that will try to get into heaven on that last day. These words might as well have been spoken by Christ just last week:

Not everyone who says to me, "Lord, Lord," will enter the kingdom of heaven, but only the one who does the will of my Father in heaven. On that day many will say to me, "Lord, Lord, did we not prophesy in your name, and cast out demons in your name, and do many deeds of power in your name?" Then I will declare to them, "I never knew you; go away from me, you evildoers."

MATTHEW 7:21-23

We could never imagine ourselves to be the people described in these verses. That would be impossible, wouldn't it? But take care of how you answer this question. The catechism weighs in heavily on this issue as well.

> The prayer of faith consists not only in saying "Lord, Lord," but in disposing the heart to do the will of the Father. Jesus calls his disciples to bring into their prayer this concern for cooperating with the divine plan. (CCC 2611)

If I told you I was casting out demons and healing people in God's name, you would probably think that I was really connected with God. And wouldn't you also think that my place in heaven was a sure thing? But this is where we have to be most careful. Jesus was talking mainly about the make-believers who are convinced that because they are working for God, they are automatically with God.

But in reality, they are using God for their own purposes. Yes, they can actually heal and help people in God's name. And yes, they can be effective and perform miracles simply because of the power inherent in God's name. But their hearts and real motives are far from Him.

Then there's the other end of the make-believer spectrum. The people Jesus is also speaking of are the ones who are sitting on the sidelines, in the back pews of churches, expecting to get into heaven simply because they haven't been all that bad during their lifetime. But they did little, if anything during their lives to promote Christ and the message of His Kingdom. Instead, they yielded to their own desires and wants, not God's.

Then there are those who are very involved in religious matters in their churches and in their communities, but with the ultimate purpose of promoting themselves, even at the expense of God's name. They love the limelight. All this may sound very judgmental but these are the words and meanings that Christ wanted us to hear. John the Baptist put it this way:

> *He must increase, but I must decrease.*
>
> JOHN 3:30

If you start hearing yourself using your name and the pronouns "I and me" more than the name of Christ in your conversations, then you're not promoting Him; you're probably using Him to promote yourself. The bottom line is very clear and simple—we always need to be in sync with God's will. The people getting into heaven are the ones who already know God and who walked and worked with Him in this life on His agenda.

Can you avoid the walk and the work? Sure, but expect to be denied entrance at the gates of heaven when you try to enter. If He doesn't recognize you as one of His own, it's all over. Are you willing to take that kind of a risk? Let me illustrate all of this with an incredible but true story.

As I write this book, it's been about three years since a fire, set by four very young boys, destroyed our offices and several other businesses located in the same building. A very weird and wonderful thing happened two days after the fire. I was walking in the middle of all the burned-out and charred remains of the building. There on the ground was a small white piece of paper seemingly untouched by the fire. I reached down and pulled it from the surrounding debris.

Unbelievably, it was my first grade catechism. I had not seen that little book in a very, very long time. It must have been buried in some box of papers we had in our archive storage in the attic of the building. It was not burned or soiled—and as if that wasn't enough, it lay opened to a page that started with the question, "Why did God make you?" Reflexively, the answer came to me even before I read it: "God made me to know Him, to love Him and to serve Him on earth and to be happy with Him forever in heaven."

Even in that scene of destruction, I could hear my first grade teacher reciting these words. Absolutely amazing! Was this a coincidence? No, it's what we might call a "God-incidence." What have we been talking about since the beginning of this book? The most important thing we do in our lives is to come to know God.

But strive first for the kingdom of God and his righteousness, and all these things will be given to you as well.

MATTHEW 6:33

When we recognize God first in all things, for any purpose, He will always hear us and respond. This is the best way to move closer to God. Once we begin to seek Him first, we will fall in love with Him. It is unavoidable. Then, as we do in other love relationships, we will want to please Him by serving Him and doing what makes Him happy.

The key is to get to know God. You can opt to keep your distance from God as I did and make all kinds of excuses why you cannot follow Him more closely, but in the end you are the one that will suffer tragically. Remember, God is the person who will operate the gate to heaven. He decides who gets in and who does not. It's imperative that He recognizes you. Finding that catechism in the fire debris hit me hard. I believe God's personal message to me was this:

"I can talk to you anywhere I choose and in many different ways. Even and especially in the midst of tragedy, I will make myself known to you and will give you what you need to know. I can preserve anything that is important to your salvation and happiness. Even though it may come through an intense blaze, I will protect it."

"As in your catechism, my message to all of you is simple. Just read it, learn it and understand it. Do not complicate it. Just follow me by coming to know me, love me and serve me. Always look for me. I am anywhere you need me. There is no place where you might go where I cannot be with you. I will always be there for you with whatever you need. Remember, it's all about eternity and spending it with me."

Have you ever wondered just how much God really wants a close relationship with each of us? It is something He talks about in the Scriptures as being good for us. It is something He truly desires more than anything else.

From the book of Saint John we see the true nature of God. This is the one of the special places in all of the Bible where God clearly reveals what He personally wants most from us more than anything else. The first quotation is from Jesus Himself. The second is from a more modern translation of Jesus' statements. Read them both very carefully and drink in the words. He is speaking directly to you.

I am the true vine, and my Father is the vinegrower. He removes every branch in me that bears no fruit. Every branch that bears fruit he prunes to make it bear more fruit. You have already been cleansed by the word that I have spoken to you. Abide in me as I abide in you. Just as the branch cannot bear fruit by itself unless it abides in the vine, neither can you unless you abide in me. I am the vine, you are the branches. Those who abide in me and I in them bear much fruit, because apart from me you can do nothing. Whoever does not abide in me is thrown away like a branch and withers; such branches are gathered, thrown into the fire, and burned. If you abide in me, and my words abide in you, ask for whatever you wish, and it will be done for you. My Father is glorified by this, that you bear much fruit and become my disciples. As the Father has loved me, so I have loved you; abide in my love. If you keep my commandments, you will abide in my love, just as I have kept my Father's commandments and abide in his love. I have said these things to you so that my joy may be in you, and that your joy may be complete.

This is my commandment, that you love one another as I have loved you. No one has greater love than this, to lay down one's life for one's friends. You are my friends if you do what I command you. I do not call you servants any longer, because the servant does not know what the master is doing; but I have called you friends, because I have made known to you everything that I have heard from my Father. You did not choose me but I chose you. And I appointed you to go and bear fruit, fruit that will last, so that the Father will give you whatever you ask him in my name. I am giving you these commands so that you may love one another.

JOHN 15:1-17

Now read the same verses as translated from *The Message.*

I am the Real Vine and my Father is the Farmer. He cuts off every branch of me that doesn't bear grapes. And every branch that is grape-bearing he prunes back so it will bear even more. You are already pruned back by the message I have spoken.

Live in me. Make your home in me just as I do in you. In the same way that a branch can't bear grapes by itself but only by being joined to the vine, you can't bear fruit unless you are joined with me.

I am the Vine, you are the branches. When you're joined with me and I with you, the relation intimate and organic, the harvest is sure to be abundant. Separated, you can't produce a thing. Anyone who separates from me is deadwood, gathered up and thrown on the bonfire. But if you make yourselves at home with me and my words are at home in you, you can be sure that whatever you ask will be listened to and acted upon. This is how my Father shows who He is—when you produce grapes, when you mature as my disciples.

I've loved you the way my Father has loved me. Make yourselves at home in my love. If you keep my commands, you'll remain intimately at home in my love. That's what I've done—kept my Father's commands and made myself at home in his love.

I've told you these things for a purpose: That my joy might be your joy, and your joy wholly mature. This is my command: Love one another the way I loved you. This is the very best way to love. Put your life on the line for your friends. You are my friends when you do the things I command you. I'm no longer calling you servants because servants don't understand what their master is thinking and planning. No, I've named you friends because I've let you in on everything I've heard from the Father.

You didn't choose me, remember; I chose you, and put you in the world to bear fruit, fruit that won't spoil. As fruit bearers, whatever you ask the Father in relation to me, He gives you.

But remember the root command: Love one another.

JOHN 15:1-17, *The Message*

These images are so personal and revealing. Did you feel God's heart? He wants us to be joined with Him in a relationship that is so intimate that it can be accurately described as a nurturing and living organic bond.

In essence, He says that we can do nothing of any long term or lasting significance without Him empowering and supporting us the whole way. It could not be described in a more meaningful and poignant manner. If this appeal from our Creator to you fails to move you closer to Him, then at least consider, for your own sake, what He says about how doomed we are without such an attachment to Him: "The Holy Spirit is like the sap of the Father's vine which bears fruit on its branches." (CCC 1108) Furthermore, if we are separated from Him, all of our own efforts will amount to nothing and we will eventually find ourselves being discarded just like deadwood.

You can opt to avoid developing a personal walking faith with God, but you will be denying God His greatest desire, which is to be intimate and close with you. Do you really want to do that to Him? And coming full circle, think of the poor Catholic. We will remain poor as long as we remain apart from Him. It's that simple.

As I said earlier, we have to get out of bed each day and choose to step onto The Road to Grace. Our choice always comes first. Our action usually precedes the response from God. He will never force us or make us come to Him. He extends His hand, His love and all of His power to aid us. We just have to accept His offer.

6

Learning to Walk with the God of the Universe

If you talk to people who have come to know God in a personal way, you'll probably have difficulty understanding and relating to their experience, unless it has happened to you too. There just isn't anything in our daily lives that can compare to meeting God. It's indescribably intimate and close. After all, we're talking about a relationship with a supernatural being. When I first realized that God was always right there with me, it produced a previously unknown kind of feeling. Things I always took for granted now looked different. My interactions with the people around me had a new sense of urgency as I wanted to share with them what I had discovered about God.

It was as if I had been visited by an angel who took me up to heaven for a thirty-minute tour. The place was so incredibly beautiful that during the whole time I was unable to speak! Then at the end of the tour I got to meet Jesus. All He said to me was, "Tell them that everything revealed to them in The Book is true." Can you imagine having such a transforming experience? What would you say to people when you returned? Even if they did believe you, what could you say?

One of my biggest difficulties has been trying to understand why people act as they do. I actually try to see their actions from

God's perspective. I can't help but wonder what motivates people to say and do things, especially when they decide to undertake highly risky activities. I have spent a great deal of time thinking about this. Then one day about eight years ago, I began to formulate a theory about how we live, a theory that to this day no one has disproved. I believe sometime ago, perhaps in the 1970's or 1980's, we stopped being Catholics, Protestants, Irish, Italian, Asian and so forth and instead all became members of the same group: the consumers.

The old labels indicating our heritage and beliefs no longer seemed functionally relevant. Because we now have so many choices before us, we have become accustomed to acting like a consumer in order to get through the day. In short, we consume whatever it is we want after we have discerned which product or choice is best for us in our situation. If you think about this, it applies to just about every aspect of our lives.

I remember a good friend of mine telling me a story about someone who came to visit him from Russia not very long ago. He took this person shopping with him at the local supermarket. The visitor just couldn't get over the amount of different products there were in each aisle. She especially marveled at all of the cereal choices. It took him over two hours to get her out of the store!

I think we do not realize what we have become—a society that simply expects to have whatever it wants, whenever it wants it. We expect a range of options in any and every situation. We want to consider all the possibilities, review the costs, and then decide which choice is best for us. We perform this routine over and over again all day long, seven days a week. Few areas of our lives are exempt from this consumer mentality.

When I began to see things more from a spiritual perspective, it became obvious that this consumerist approach had also made its way into our dealings with God. We just cannot accept the fact that there could only be one God, with no other alternatives. We think that there has to be at least a few choices. Why? Because that's the way it is with most everything else! So in order to deal effectively with this "only one God limit," we feel it necessary to re-make Him. Instead of us being born again, it is Christ or God who gets reborn. Every day we custom-build a new God or a new version of Jesus Christ to suit our own needs. We think that God has to give us whatever we ask for because we're the consumers, the ones with all the buying power.

If He doesn't answer our prayers and requests as we like, we'll often just go ahead and take what we want, claiming that God probably meant to give it to us anyway. We're so used to having things as we want them, we now assume God means for us to have most anything we want.

We reconstruct Him and His rules so that He is now more user-friendly, pliable and willing to see things from our perspective. He will even "cut us more slack" when we get into trouble. And the best part is that we can each have a "Jesus" built to our own specifications and needs. We can also modify Him and His rules from day to day to adjust to sudden changes in our personal needs and wants.

Chapter 32 of Exodus tells the story of the golden calf and God's reaction to the idolatry of the Israelites. While Moses went off to speak with God and receive the Ten Commandments, the people became restless and impatient. So they created another more accessible and responsive god in the form of a golden calf. To say the least, neither Moses nor God was happy with them and God dealt with the Israelites most severely.

There are many parallels in this story to our present-day situation. We, like the Israelites, have adopted many idols of our own whether they be in the form of money, wealth or leisure activities. We literally worship these things and look for them before looking for God. Read Exodus 32 and ask yourself the question, "If God dealt with these people in this fashion, why wouldn't He do the same with us today?" It's a good question to think about.

This trend toward "custom-building God" became more obvious to me as I counseled more and more people in financial difficulty. People were suspending the rules of moral and spiritual behavior as they tried to work out of their difficulties. And this tendency is still prevalent in our culture. This was a huge revelation to me and it staggered me even more when I realized that I have been guilty of this behavior as much as anyone else. Consider what happens most every time we drive our cars.

Many of us are immediately faced with a choice to either obey the rules of the road or suspend those rules, "just for this one time." The speed limit says forty-five mph so that means we can do fifty-five or sixty mph, does it not? And because so many of us do this on a regular basis, it no longer seems like a crime or even an infraction of the law. So the rules, in whatever particular area of concern, are flexible according to our needs or mood at the time. I could not think of a more dangerous way to live.

But coming to know God as a personal friend changed all of this for me and the changes that followed could accurately be described as a series of shocks, for I found that His ways are not similar to my ways:

> *For my thoughts are not your thoughts, nor are your ways my ways, says the* LORD.
>
> ISAIAH 55:8

As a friend, He sticks pretty close to us and sees what we are thinking and doing every day. His presence grew in my life and I had an increasingly hard time suspending any of His rules to suit my needs and desires.

He was not as I had imagined Him in my earlier days growing

up as a Catholic. Once again, I had always thought that God was too busy to notice the "small stuff" in my life. I thought He was concerned only with the bigger picture and world issues. But I was wrong! He lives in the details of our lives. This is where we prove or disprove the claims we make about God. If we love Him, then we will do what He expects of us even in the privacy of our cars and driving habits.

If you think about it, wherever Jesus went in the Gospels, He surprised and shocked most everyone because, like us, they too convinced themselves that God was something He really was not. Christ had to straighten them out. As a matter of fact the entire Old Testament is littered with story after story of how God "straightened out" the Israelites.

It's not easy to live your life within a given set of religious beliefs for so many years and then find out that much of what you thought and believed just was not true. I've changed many of my personal opinions on things simply because I am now working to see the world more from God's point of view than my own. God will open our eyes to the truth if we'll let Him.

I believe this "re-creation of God" phenomenon stems in part from the Catholic Church's organizational structure and how it has evolved over time. The diagram below shows how God's relationship with many Catholics has had to come through the institution of the Catholic Church itself.

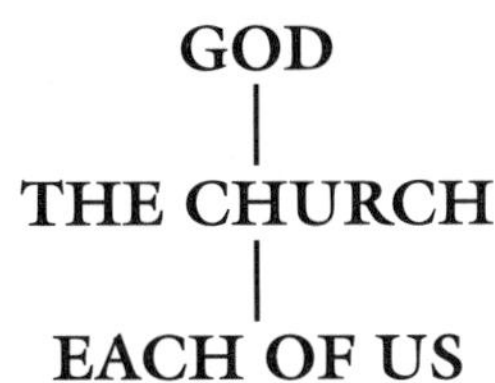

This has worked well up to a point. As the Church developed over the years, it grew in a way that at times caused it to become a filter for what God was saying to His people. In positioning itself between God and us, it seeks to act as a facilitator for helping us develop our faith with God. But as is the case with any filtering device, it can sometimes act as a block if it is not maintained and cleaned regularly.

As a result of factors like bureaucratic structuring and internal politics, the Church at times has impeded the growth of peoples' faith. But this is typical of many large organizations. Consequently, some Catholics perceive that to develop a personal bond with God, they must first go through the Church. As a result, Catholics have become accustomed to the idea of not having to deal with God directly.

It certainly seems easier to have a priest or clergy member interpret what God is saying, deal with God for us and then come back and tell us what we need to hear and do. As a consequence, we as parishioners have been let off the hook, so to speak, as to what our responsibilities to God, the Church and one another have been over the years. We have relied solely on the clergy for too much and for too long. So it's no surprise that many Catholics still think that being a good Catholic means that all you have to do is go to church and "show up, listen up and pay up" when necessary. Too often, too many of us have come to rely too heavily on the Church itself for all of our spiritual needs.

Take a look at another model that would enhance not only Church life in every aspect, but would also bring each of us into that deep and personal walking faith with God, which is what He seeks.

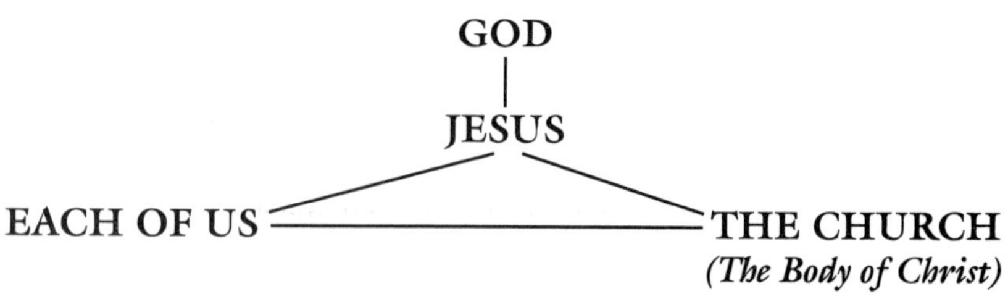

The left side of the diagram is where we develop that personal link and bond with Christ as is spoken of in Saint John's Gospel.

Very truly, I tell you, no one can see the kingdom of God without being born from above.

JOHN 3:3

Saint John encourages us to forge a new relationship with God, through Jesus Christ. As Catholics, we need to be born again and develop that walking faith with Him just like each of the Disciples did some 2000 years ago. This is the piece that has been missing from Catholicism for too many Catholics, for too many years.

On the right side of the diagram, the Church continues in its direct relationship with God through Jesus Christ, but now it changes to the extent that it becomes a newly infused Body of Christ. How? Because as the Holy Spirit continues to work directly between God and the Church, He can now also work more freely between each of us and the Body of Christ. The Holy Spirit Himself can now move freely between God, the Church and us. We have to be available on a personal level with God and accessible to the Spirit, just as each of the original followers of Christ were as they waited for Pentecost.

When we allow God to have personal access to each one of us, we in turn can carry the effects of our newfound relationship with God back into the Body. This will energize and empower the people in the Church.

This could lead to a revival or renewal of faith, not only in Catholicism but throughout all of Christianity. Notice that the flow lines indicate that this new bonding experience runs back and forth amongst all three entities more freely than it does perhaps right now. This triangular model works to everyone's benefit and interestingly, it is of the most benefit to God Himself.

Why? Because this model will greatly increase the probability that more of His children will find their way home to Him (see John 6:39).

In summary, God will now have greater access to each of us personally, through His Church as He does now and throughout the Body of Christ as each newly energized and born from above individual interacts in their local churches. Additionally, this plan helps eliminate any organizationally generated blocking structures or filters that may develop in the Church.

We as Catholics should begin to realize that we can no longer sit back and let someone else provide us with salvation. Each of us must find Jesus as each of the twelve Disciples did, commit ourselves to Him and start getting to know Him again. We can then come home to our Church and help take care of it and those who will look to join it in the future.

This proposal may frighten many who are in the Church hierarchy but it shouldn't. If anything, it should help the Church grow in a world that desperately needs the structure of the Catholic Church as well as the guidance of the Holy Spirit. We have the chance to promote and facilitate personal spiritual growth amongst Catholics as they learn to interact with God Himself. Since God is giving us the chance to make these changes, if we do nothing to promote this combination of a personal and corporate approach to God, then we can expect God to deal very harshly with us when the time comes.

There's something else that's very important to God—and it has special relevance to our society today. It's our wealth and how we utilize it. Being in the financial services industry, what God taught me in this area has had a profound affect on me.

Why should we be so blessed here in America while elsewhere around the world (and even within our own borders) people are desperate for the bare essentials of life? This was one of my first big questions on my walk with God and He answered me very quickly.

In America we are blessed because we have asked to be blessed. Over the years many came to this country and prayed for God to pour out His blessings on them. You can hear it in the lyrics of patriotic songs like "America the Beautiful" and "God Bless America." Well, He answered those prayers with the incredible outpouring of resources and talented people we call America. But then something else happened. We never stopped asking for more.

We do help a lot of people around the world and in our own communities every day, but that level of aid has not kept pace with the level of blessings we receive from God. Especially in the last twenty years, our focus has shifted more and more to our own needs and wants first. We have been asking Him for so much for so long, that we don't know any other way of behaving in front of Him. We see Him as being here mainly to shower us with His bounty. And now it seems to have gone even further.

Many of us have stopped asking and just expect that God will continue to give us what we want, regardless of how we behave toward Him and those around us. I believe that in the eyes of God, we've become spoiled. That's also how many people around the world perceive Americans—and why some have come to hate us. They see us as being spoiled with the majority of the world's wealth and resources, which we spend mostly on ourselves.

Yes, God wants to bless us with what we need and even many of the things we want. But He first wants us to be servants and stewards to those around us—just as He Himself was while here on earth. He wants us to give to others and at the same time live in such a way as to make being a Catholic and a Christian inviting to others.

We hear a great deal about how some Christians "go over the edge" in their thinking and form cult-like groups or even a hate-based theology. But we seldom hear the simple truth that Jesus professed and declared. He commanded us to just love one another, even if that other person hates you or you don't approve of their lifestyle. Show them the love of Christ in all of your actions toward them. Then you will be blameless in God's eyes. However, in contrast to this, the current approach to God for many of us is the ultimate form of consumerism and couldn't be any more opposite to the way He wants us to behave. We have created many golden calves—SUV's, exotic vacations, second homes and so forth—to replace our one true God.

Many of these things are not bad in themselves, but we put the bulk of our discretionary energies and financial resources into a focused pursuit and maintenance of these luxuries instead of the things that concern God the most. This is where He will hold us most accountable. In His eyes, we are a wealthy people in terms of resources and access to services. Jesus said,

> *From everyone to whom much has been given, much will be required; and from the one to whom much has been entrusted, even more will be demanded.*
>
> LUKE 12:48

Few verses of Scripture frighten me more than this one because I know that in God's eyes, I am a rich man—and not just monetarily. The more resources, gifts, talents and understanding I have, the greater is my responsibility to use them effectively for God. Someday, not too far in the future, God will ask me for an accounting of how I spent the wealth, resources and talents that He entrusted to me (see the Parable of the Talents in Matthew 25:14-30). I hope I'll be able to answer Him well.

Remember, He's not asking us to give away everything we own. He's asking us to hold our wealth and resources loosely in our hands so that when others around us are in real need, we can cheerfully part with some of our blessings. Those are the times when we can be most like Christ Himself. Consider this—who did He touch most profoundly during His ministry? It was those who were in extreme need, the sick, lame and possessed. We, who have so much, have the same opportunity to touch others. Interestingly enough, Jesus gave all that He did to the people of His day without giving them any money.

Here's where we can see the Road to Grace as a two-way street. God provides many of us with much more than we need so that we can share those resources with those who are in need. The Road to Grace is designed so that we can bring others along with us. That's its greatest purpose! We're all supposed to get home on that road. As we walk along it, we will see many people lost and hurting. Some may not be far from the road but others will be. God will tell us whom to help. But it's important to wait for His lead in those situations. Too many well-meaning people have gotten entangled in other peoples' problems because they did not wait for God to instruct them.

This brings up the topic of how involved we should become in the problems and issues in other peoples' lives. There is no hard and fast rule to guide us in this area, except to remember that we always need to keep in close contact with God. If you think about it, He is the only one who knows specifically how to help those in need around you. He will also guide you as to how far to go in helping others. This is another very practical reason for maintaining a close walking faith with Him.

The bottom line is this: We cannot be consumers where God is concerned. We only get to make one choice. It's either His will or ours. This may sound restrictive and confining but it isn't. His will for us provides for many of the things we want. He just eliminates the things we want that can harm us in the end. In the long run, it's the best deal a person can hope for. On top of everything else, God promises to provide us with an incredible eternal retirement plan. You just cannot beat it.

Approximately one year after reading *In His Steps*, I became convinced that if I was to continue to develop this friendship with God, I would have to do it directly through Christ. He was the part that was missing in my religious upbringing and was still missing in my life. I couldn't go any further without recognizing Him as the way into heaven. I had to make a decision about Jesus Christ, as we all do at some point in our lives. Up until then, I had never checked Him out for myself. I never took the initiative and researched the reality of God for myself.

I came to realize that I had been leaning on the Catholic Church for too long as the sole provider for my salvation. I was assuming that I was saved simply because I was sitting in a Catholic Church on certain Sundays, going to Communion and complying with God's laws as I saw fit.

I presumed that in the end, I would somehow make it into heaven. It is my guess that most Catholics believe this very same thing, if they're even thinking about these issues at all. Since we do not talk about this topic publicly, it's very hard to gauge where people stand on their expectations concerning heaven.

But I do know we're making one person happy by not talking about God and eternal life. And that person is Satan. Satan wants us to live our lives half asleep, when it comes to matters of faith and God. He does not want us talking about these issues for fear that we'll wake up and see the reality of our plight. He'll even approve of us going to church, as long as we don't wake up and realize how much eternal danger we are headed toward. Satan is happiest when we think and act like the make-believers. This is his greatest fraud of all.

Because the "Catholic crowd" is going in a certain direction, many people just assume it's the right path and just follow along. They don't think for themselves. They're too busy to even try. Since many do not have a personal walking faith with God, they will likely get lost in the end. For me, I decided that I had to find

Christ and go to Him myself. I finally realized that this was something that basically involved only God and me. But this realization did not make me want to change religions or leave the Catholic Church, as it has with many other people. Instead, to this day, I always return from my times with God re-energized looking for ways to help my Catholic brothers and sisters see Christ on that critical personal level.

Finally, I realized too that I was no longer the "owner" of everything in my life, but rather the steward or custodian of the treasures God had entrusted to me. It was a major shift in my perspective of the things that were under my control and responsibility—so major that I came to see the relationships He had placed in my life as being more important than wealth or possessions. I was the steward of those precious relationships and I needed to nurture them. I am deeply committed to some of my relationships but most are shallow at best. But in every case, I am to show my love for all those I encounter every day. This is the biggest challenge for any Christian because as you know, some people can be very hard to love.

God decided to teach me how to love by opening my eyes to the truth of the most crucial verses of Scripture in the Bible. Before we can change our behavior, we have to understand God. This is where the Bottom Line Scriptures come into the picture. And it's our next stop on the Road to Grace.

7

The Bottom Line Scriptures: The Core of God's Message

As I've mentioned, solutions and answers that really work are highly sought after these days. When I counsel people with financial difficulties, I usually don't get to meet with them more than once or twice. So I have to be ready with whatever answers they need. Jesus had the same challenge in His ministry. He was constantly moving from place to place, without the luxury of helping them work through their problems over time.

But simple, concise solutions to life's problems are hard to come by. Politicians and leaders of organizations seldom are willing to summarize things simply and concisely because life is complicated and every situation has extenuating circumstances. And remember too that we are consumers at heart. We want to have a variety of solutions available for every problem. So it's not easy to deliver the "bottom line"—an answer to a given problem that's boiled down to just one observation or statement.

With all this in mind, I followed God on a journey through what I call some of the "Bottom Line Scriptures" in the Bible. They tell us how God sees the options for living a good life and make it clear as to what is most important to Him. God led me through them; now we'll explore them together.

8

Bottom Line #1: The Real Bottom Line

One of the things I most appreciate about the Gospels is how Jesus always got to the heart of the questions people were asking Him. For instance, there was a Pharisee of the law who tried to test Jesus by asking Him to sum up all the laws and rules found in the Hebrew law in one short, concise rule. There were at least six hundred and thirteen individual statutes during those days. I believe this was a critical moment for Christ because it was His opportunity to give us the fundamental blueprint for getting into heaven. And in spite of the enormity of the task, He did it.

He summed up all the laws into just two overriding commandments and ways of behaving. Read these words from Matthew's account:

> *When the Pharisees heard that he had silenced the Sadducees, they gathered together, and one of them, a lawyer, asked him a question to test him. "Teacher, which commandment in the law is the greatest?" He said to him, "'You shall love the Lord your God with all your heart, and with all your soul, and with all your mind.' This is the greatest and first commandment. And a second is like it: 'You shall love your neighbor as yourself.' On these two commandments hang all the law and the prophets."*
>
> MATTHEW 22:34-40

How many times have we heard this Scripture quoted at Mass? I have to admit that over the years I'd given it little thought. Why is it that we can hear the most critical truths of our faith and essentially yawn when we do? I believe it's because we don't make these words part of our life goals each day, we do not live them. But I also think the problem goes even deeper. We no longer even know what the words mean.

However, on my journey with God, these words took on new meaning. I came to see them as Christ meant them; I came to see them through His eyes. For example, long ago I could speak Italian to a certain degree. Today, I can't. When I hear the words now, they are somewhat familiar but I cannot get any meaning from the sentences. The same thing happens when we stop using and living God's words. We can hear them all we want, but we must apply them frequently in our lives for them to have a long-term beneficial effect on us.

Matthew 22:34-40 is considered by many to be foundational to the Christian faith—and I've come to some conclusions about what Jesus had to say here. I think it's much easier to love God than our neighbor. If someone tells me that he loves God, then who am I to say that he doesn't? It would be difficult at best to prove that he does not. So, I would have to accept the statement. But loving those around us is another story. We have to take them as they are, with all of their "rough edges." Ungrateful relatives and employees, bitter ex-spouses and children, customers that won't pay you, bosses that take advantage of you—they all make the commandment to "love your neighbor as yourself" nearly impossible to comply with.

So eventually, many of us give up on this commandment and focus more on pleasing God by doing things like going to Church regularly and being nice to the people we like or who think as we do. We like to think that if we at least do a good job complying with the first commandment, then God will be happy enough with our efforts. Right? Wrong! Read what the Gospel writer Saint John said about loving God and loving others:

Those who say, "I love God," and hate their brothers or sisters, are liars; for those who do not love a brother or sister whom they have seen, cannot love God whom they have not seen. The commandment we have from him is this: those who love God must love their brothers and sisters also.

1 JOHN 4:20-21

You cannot fulfill the first commandment to love God until you've obeyed the second, and seemingly harder-to-comply-with, commandment to love those around you. Here's how the catechism explains this verse with regard to our receiving God's mercy and grace:

"Now—and this is daunting—this outpouring of mercy cannot penetrate our hearts as long as we have not forgiven those who have trespassed against us. *Love, like the Body of Christ, is indivisible*; we cannot love the God we cannot see if we do not love the brother or sister we do see. In refusing to forgive our brothers and sisters, our hearts are closed and their hardness makes them *impervious* to the Father's merciful love; but in confessing our sins, our hearts are opened to his grace."

(CCC 2840, emphasis added)

Perhaps now you can see how important this verse is to our faith walk. Many of us go around thinking we're working effectively for God and often wonder why we don't have more energy and success in our ministries.

Could it be that we haven't dealt with an old hatred or disagreement with someone (see Matthew 5:23-24)? If we haven't, it may be preventing God's grace and power from reaching us and aiding us in our work.

It's impossible to make those around us easier to love. We have to live with them as they are and slowly work at helping them see the correct point of view—God's. But while working at this, we may have to admit we are wrong with regard to a particular issue. Many of us do not like admitting we're wrong, much less being forced to change our habits and ways of thinking. And because we do not like confrontation and change, we may purposely stay away from others who need our help.

So where is God most likely to test us? I believe it comes in how we treat the people we encounter in our daily lives, especially the ones that are hurting and needy. In other words, how much do we really care about all of the people around us? Not an easy question to answer, is it?

But just as you begin to wrestle with a question such as that, God takes us to an even deeper personal level. Can we love God and one another while not loving ourselves? Do we even know what it means to love ourselves?

Jesus tells us in Matthew 22:39 *"You shall love your neighbor as yourself."* He doesn't explain it or even expand on it. It's as if He just assumes we would know what He's talking about because it's in our nature to always be good to ourselves. And it seems He further assumes that we can use that love we have for ourselves, as a model for how to treat others around us.

I wonder how significant it is, in God's eyes, that we must now question even our own motives and reasons for loving ourselves. What happens if we lose that reference point? What if we no longer care about ourselves? Is it still possible to care deeply about others or even God? Remember, the opposite of love is not hate but apathy, or not caring. Saint Paul gives us the beginning of an answer to these questions.

Or do you not know that your body is a temple of the Holy Spirit within you, which you have from God, and that you are not your own? For you were bought with a price; therefore glorify God in your body.

1 Corinthians 6:19-20

The very notion that our bodies can act as a temple for God's Holy Spirit can be an unsettling revelation to many of us. We live in an age in which we each have rights—especially the right to do what we want with our own bodies. To find out now that God has a claim on our bodies may not be a welcomed thought to many people.

As Catholics, when we receive our Confirmation, we are allowing God to inhabit our bodies, minds, hearts and souls. We are literally yielding over to Him our control of these areas. I'm afraid that many Catholics (and Christians in general for that matter) never understood this fact when they made their Confirmation as children. Many of us probably thought it was just another religious ceremony that was a necessary part of our faith experience, and indeed it is. But the critical fact that many miss is that since God's Spirit now resides in the innermost parts of our being, we can no longer do things with our bodies that are not compatible with His Spirit. We are to keep our "temples" clean and free from sin because God's Holy Spirit cannot co-exist with anything that's not of God. If I am vigilant to not let anything impure into my life, then God's Spirit can grow in my "temple" and I can become born anew (see John 3:3). This gives me the ability to effectively love God and those around me. His Spirit lives in me and knows me, a most important detail come judgment day.

When we agree to step onto the Road to Grace, all of this should gradually become obvious to us. It's just another way of looking at the process of salvation. And don't miss the point that Saint Paul makes here. We were "purchased at a price" and therefore are not our own. By the very act of Christ's death, the redemption of our souls gives ownership back to God. He bought us and therefore owns us.

However, if this idea offends you, then it is something you can opt to avoid. Once more, you can use your free will to reject this concept of ownership. God gives us our free will, so the choice is up to you and you alone.

But it's often not that easy to see this rejection taking place. We don't normally wake up one day saying "I do not want the Holy Spirit using me as His temple!" Instead it may occur in a more insidious way when we slowly allow things God despises into our minds and hearts where they take root and establish permanent residency. When this happens the Holy Spirit leaves our temples. He no longer lives within us because we have chosen something His nature is not compatible with. It may be drugs, alcohol, pornography, or some other serious sin. But in every case the result is the same; we grieve or offend the Holy Spirit and chase Him away from us.

Truly I tell you, people will be forgiven for their sins and whatever blasphemies they utter; but whoever blasphemes against the Holy Spirit can never have forgiveness, but is guilty of an eternal sin.

MARK 3:28-29

God's words tell us that if we reject His Holy Spirit, then we will not be forgiven. Why? Because we are showing him we *want* to stay away from His Holy Spirit. Using our free will, this is a choice we make against having God within us.

Whenever we get into any kind of substance abuse, whether it is physical or psychological, we've chosen to abuse His temple within us. It sends a clear signal to God that we no longer want Him present. So we cannot be pardoned since we do not seek His forgiveness. Absolution is a process that we have to initiate.

Think about what athletes go through to train for an Olympic event. They are very careful to keep their bodies free from anything that would be a detriment to their health. This is how we are to be with God, pure and clean.

We started this discussion with learning about how important it is to first love God. We soon found out that loving God was something intimately tied to loving our brothers and sisters as well. But now we find out that unless we strive through prayer and right living, to keep our "temples of the Holy Spirit" clean and free from immoral behavior, all of our efforts at following Christ will be in vain. Just as Jesus worked hard to keep His Spirit synchronized with His Father's Spirit while here on earth, we too are to keep our spirits in line with His. Any behavior on our part that shows we do not care what happens to us, can be a clear sign that we do not love ourselves. For example, we must be so careful not to over-extend ourselves each day by working too hard. God does call certain people to be martyrs but not that many. We are called to love and care for ourselves, so we can do the same for God and those around us. Do you remember how Jesus cleared the Temple of all the money changers (see Mark 11:15-19)? As He did this, He said:

Is it not written, "My house shall be called a house of prayer for all the nations"? But you have made it a den of robbers.

MARK 11:17

This is deeply symbolic of our need to clear our own temples of those habits and ideas that are not in line with God.

Isn't it interesting? Our culture today is focused on giving each of us all kinds of pleasure and meeting personal needs but even with all this attention, we can still see how poor we really are. Without God's Holy Spirit we truly are poor Catholics. It's the one thing many of us are missing. And Jesus said it plainly:

The Poor Catholic

I am the vine, you are the branches. Those who abide in me and I in them bear much fruit, because apart from me you can do nothing.

John 15:5

No matter how you look at it, our faith in God starts with us. If God is the footings to our faith, then we are the ones that have to give God our approval to pour those footings in our lives. The first step then in building a faith in God is for us to come to Him and acknowledge Him as our Lord as well as our Savior. As we seek Him further, we will become aware of one incredible fact: how precious we are to Him.

He died for each one of us. If there was only one person ever created in all of time, I am convinced that Jesus would still have offered Himself on the cross as payment for the sins of that one person. There is nothing more precious in your life than the gift God gave you, of your own life. Never abuse it or take it for granted. With these "temples of His Holy Spirit," we can achieve a great deal for God and for others.

9

Bottom Line #2: Speaking Directly

When Jesus spoke to the people of His day, He very often used parables and stories to get His message across to them. Some people at the time may have felt that it was difficult to understand exactly what He meant. But in the book of Matthew, chapter 25, verses 31-46, Jesus spoke to all of us in no uncertain terms. To me, it is one of the most crucial bottom line statements in the entire Bible. Talking about the Final Judgment, Jesus leaves no doubt as to what will happen on that last day:

When the Son of Man comes in his glory, and all the angels with him, then he will sit on the throne of his glory. All the nations will be gathered before him, and he will separate people one from another as a shepherd separates the sheep from the goats, and he will put the sheep at his right hand and the goats at the left. Then the king will say to those at his right hand, "Come, you that are blessed by my Father, inherit the kingdom prepared for you from the foundation of the world; for I was hungry and you gave me food, I was thirsty and you gave me something to drink, I was a stranger and you welcomed me, I was naked and you gave me clothing, I was sick and you took care of me, I was in prison and you visited me." Then the righteous will answer him, "Lord, when was it that we saw you hungry and gave you food, or thirsty and gave you something to drink? And when was it that we saw you a stranger and welcomed you, or naked and gave you clothing? And when was it that we saw you sick or in prison and visited you?" And the king will answer them, "Truly I tell you, just as you did it to one of the least of these who are members of my family, you did it to me." Then he will say to those at his left hand, "You that are accursed, depart from me into the eternal fire prepared for the devil and his angels; for I was hungry and you gave me no food, I was thirsty and you gave me nothing to drink, I was a stranger and you did not welcome me, naked and you did not give me clothing, sick and in prison and you did not visit me." Then they also will answer, "Lord, when was it that we saw you hungry or thirsty or a stranger or naked or sick or in prison, and did not take care of you?" Then he will answer them, "Truly I tell you, just as you did not do it to one of the least of these, you did not do it to me." And these will go away into eternal punishment, but the righteous into eternal life.

MATTHEW 25:31-46

What I find so interesting about this passage is not only its crystal-clear meaning but also its lack of any mention of those who were good husbands and mothers who cared for their families, went to church regularly, went to Communion and Confession and so forth. Why aren't these people and their good works mentioned?

I believe the answer is that God assumes that we will normally and automatically care for our families, attend church and so forth. Our reward in heaven comes to us not because we didn't hurt others or because we did not abuse our children or employees, but because we went out of our way to show our love and concern for those that need our help. The bottom line is that if there are people near us who are in need, then we should go and help them. It isn't any more complicated than that and it's exactly what Jesus did in His ministry here on earth.

10

Bottom Line #3: How Then Should We Live?

Consider another major bottom line Scripture in the story of the Good Samaritan:

Just then a lawyer stood up to test Jesus. "Teacher," he said, "what must I do to inherit eternal life?" He said to him, "What is written in the law? What do you read there?" He answered, "You shall love the Lord your God with all your heart, and with all your soul, and with all your strength, and with all your mind; and your neighbor as yourself." And he said to him, "You have given the right answer; do this, and you will live."

But wanting to justify himself, he asked Jesus, "And who is my neighbor?" Jesus replied, "A man was going down from Jerusalem to Jericho, and fell into the hands of robbers, who stripped him, beat him, and went away, leaving him half dead. Now by chance a priest was going down that road; and when he saw him, he passed by on the other side. So likewise a Levite, when he came to the place and saw him, passed by on the other side. But a Samaritan while traveling came near him; and when he saw him, he was moved with pity. He went to him and bandaged his wounds, having poured oil and wine on them. Then he put him on his own animal, brought him to an inn, and took care of him. The next day he took out two denarii, gave them to the innkeeper, and said, 'Take care of him; and when I come back, I will repay you whatever more you spend.' Which of these three, do you think, was a neighbor to the man who fell into the hands of the robbers?" He said, "The one who showed him mercy." Jesus said to him, "Go and do likewise."

LUKE 10:25-37

Here is another of Christ's stories whose meaning is clear, straightforward and unmistakable. Jesus specifically answers the question as to who our neighbors are and how we are to treat them. In the mind of Christ, our response to those in need is simple: Care for them. God not only wants us to be closely connected to Him, but also to love the people He puts in our lives. This is critical. If what God is saying here is true, then it means that we may have to give up things like our Saturday golf game and instead spend time with a friend, co-worker or employee, trying to help him or her with their personal problems and needs. While we deserve a little time to ourselves to relax and enjoy life, and while many of us just hate getting involved in other peoples' personal problems, this is exactly where God wants us to go.

But again, I will caution you on this point. Before you can help anyone in their personal struggles or problems, you must first make certain of your own grounding. This is another prime reason why we need to have that personal contact with God. When we go to help those in our lives, we really do not know for sure what is best for them. But God does. He sees everything present, past and future. If we are well connected with His Holy Spirit, and we know He wants us to help someone in particular who is close to us, then He will give us the right advice to pass along.

It's almost as if we become a conduit or pipe delivering God's word to those He directs to us. He wants us to connect with Him and then connect with others. But never, ever go out on this kind of endeavor without that all critical primary connection to God. Without it, you will fail and can do great damage to the person you are trying to help. But the word "love" today means little of what it meant in Jesus' day.

There is no better illustration of the true meaning of the word love than in the sacrifice that Christ made for us on the cross. Everything He told His Disciples and those that follow Him is based on this kind of love. For Jesus, love means that we are to "pour ourselves" into one another. Because of his real love for us, He poured out His life for us at Calvary.

Maybe it would be more relevant to substitute the word invest for the word love, to best describe it in today's terms. It would seem more accurate to say that we are to invest ourselves in others, would it not? When you invest in something, you take your resources and put them at risk in order to reap a gain or a profit later on. The Good Samaritan invested his own money and time in helping the sick person get well. What Christ did on the cross was, in a sense, the ultimate investment of all time. I believe that He expects us to do the same for those in need whom we come across every day. That's what He is telling us to do in Matthew 25.

As in the world of finance, investing in other people is at best a risky business. The profit comes when those we help can see Christ in our actions and come to know Him on a personal level. That's what we call glorifying God. All of the Scriptures we've discussed so far instruct us to devote ourselves to the welfare of other people. This is the great lesson God teaches us and expects us to follow—because that is exactly what He did for us. He invested Himself in us. Has there ever been another time in human history where the need to "spend" something of ourselves on others—instead of acquiring more and more things for ourselves—was greater?

Consider this: Jesus told us that the greatest act we can perform is to love God and others. Looking at it from a reverse angle, the opposite of love is not hate, but rather apathy and indifference. When we exhibit a lack of concern for those around us because we're too busy or involved in our own things, we are actually doing the exact opposite of what God wants from us. We are ignoring those He brings to us for care and attention. We become like the Priest and the Levite in the story of the Good Samaritan.

This is how we are losing contact with one another today. Relationships thrive on love, communication, concern and personal attention. When we either don't care or feel that we cannot afford to care about others, our love for one another will grow cold.

And because of the increase of lawlessness, the love of many will grow cold.

MATTHEW 24:12

While it is impossible to help everyone we encounter in a day, it is the attitude we display toward others that matters. Is it in our nature to want to help others or do we try to avoid being forced to lend a hand? I believe this is how God will ultimately judge us. He will look into our hearts and see what feelings we have for others and what habits come naturally to us. If we cultivate love in our hearts, then it will show outwardly in our actions with others. The habits and lifestyle we create for ourselves, because of that love, will leave a clear imprint of that truth in our hearts. It will be easy for God to see if love is the chief motivating force in our hearts or not.

There is one more thing to consider about Matthew 24:12. The behavior it describes will occur mainly in the end times. It tells us that as we approach the time of Christ's second coming, our love and compassion for one another will diminish greatly. We don't know for sure when that time will come but we do know for certain that time is running out. So remember this fact: The keys to heaven are carried by the people you meet each day. Invest yourself in your neighbors. It is the way you will gain heaven.

11

Bottom Line #4: Going Home

But what holds us back from complying fully with these words of Christ? If these Scriptures are true and come directly from God, then why do we have such difficulty complying with even the simplest of God's commands? The answer is that if we allow ourselves to be directly confronted with the biblical truths that God has expressed to us and if we acknowledge these truths to be factually true in our minds and hearts, then we would be forced into making a choice concerning God. It would either be for Him or against Him and that choice would have to extend to every aspect of our lives. But again, only two choices are far too few for our consumerist tastes. If, for example, we were to agree with God on the matter of loving others, then we would have to begin treating people as He treated them.

Think about how much time Jesus spent with the people He encountered. He was with them a great deal, doing all He could to heal and teach them. How many of us are prepared to make a similar investment of our time, love and personal resources in our friends, co-workers, employees, creditors, suppliers, people that don't think like us, and even our enemies. For many of us, it would require a permanent radical change in the way we think and act toward God and others.

Again, it's the concept of stepping onto the Road to Grace and allowing God to have a greater influence in our daily lives. We need to seek a closeness with God to the point where we live with Him in our thoughts and feelings. The result is that He begins to affect our actions. I believe that our bodies, minds and souls would resonate in agreement with the Father as we continue to live and work according to His will.

I also believe that we each have something like a "spiritual homing device" that directs us back to our Father. But our wills resist this kind of move. Some of us work too hard at our worldly jobs and concerns, to the point where they consume much of our thoughts and energy, "disabling" that homing device and diverting us from finding our way back to God. That's why the rest of us have to be available to show others the way back home.

Worldly preoccupations aside, it's most often our pride and will that prevent us from yielding to God and behaving the way He expects. Consequently, this keeps us from complying with His most basic and fundamental commandments, to love God and each other. The more we focus on our wants, the less we'll be able to see God in our lives.

Read now the account of the prodigal son. This is a most revealing story in that it shows us the true nature of God's heart. In so many ways, it also represents exactly where many of us now are in relation to God. As you read this, ask yourself which son are you?

There was a man who had two sons. The younger of them said to his father, "Father, give me the share of the property that will belong to me." So he divided his property between them. A few days later the younger son gathered all he had and traveled to a distant country, and there he squandered his property in dissolute living. When he had spent everything, a severe famine took place throughout that country, and he began to be in need. So he went and hired himself out to one of the citizens of that country, who sent him to his fields to feed the pigs. He would gladly have filled himself with the pods that the pigs were eating; and no one gave him anything. But when he came to himself he said, "How many of my father's hired hands have bread enough and to spare, but here I am dying of hunger! I will get up and go to my father, and I will say to him, 'Father, I have sinned against heaven and before you; I am no longer worthy to be called your son; treat me like one of your hired hands.'" So he set off and went to his father. But while he was still far off, his father saw him and was filled with compassion; he ran and put his arms around him and kissed him. Then the son said to him, "Father, I have sinned against heaven and before you; I am no longer worthy to be called your son." But the father said to his slaves, "Quickly, bring out a robe—the best one—and put it on him; put a ring on his finger and sandals on his feet. And get the fatted calf and kill it, and let us eat and celebrate; for this son of mine was dead and is alive again; he was lost and is found!" And they began to celebrate.

LUKE 15:11-24

This is a story about conversion and God's unconditional love. A delinquent son sees the error in his thinking and in his actions. He also realizes that his father was right all along and now is ready to return to him and admit that he was wrong. He is also willing to change his ways. The father, for his part, is eagerly waiting for him to return. But this story also demonstrates to us the great key to Christianity: We can receive forgiveness regardless of what we have done and as long as we are truly contrite and will no longer engage in that sin.

God will accept us back even when we do the most horrible things. *But*, we have to change our ways. That's what it means to repent. We cannot continue to live as we did. The prodigal son came home and stayed home. He did not go off again and return to his wicked lifestyle.

We should take great encouragement from these verses because we do have a Father in heaven that is eagerly waiting for us to return to Him. All we have to do is to begin to turn back to Him. As soon as He sees our intention is to return to Him, He'll come to us quickly and embrace us with His love.

Please do not miss this critical point—the prodigal son was lost and in his father's eyes, he was dead. He wasn't just away on vacation, having a good time while everyone expected him to eventually come home. He was lost and in grave danger of never again seeing his father. The father wasn't sure that his son would ever come back. In other words he was on the road to death and destruction (see Matthew 7:13-14). He was lost.

The way home to heaven is accomplished by being one with God and working to help our brothers and sisters find their way home as well.

12

Bottom Line #5: It's About Children

It wasn't long into my walk with the Lord before He showed me something else that is exceedingly important to Him. While He makes it clear in His Word that we are to love God and one another, He also mentions a certain group of people who are extremely precious to Him: children. Back in the time of Jesus, children, like women, were viewed as being only a little more valuable than livestock. But read what Jesus says about children:

At that time the disciples came to Jesus and asked, "Who is the greatest in the kingdom of heaven?" He called a child, whom he put among them, and said, "Truly I tell you, unless you change and become like children, you will never enter the kingdom of heaven. Whoever becomes humble like this child is the greatest in the kingdom of heaven. Whoever welcomes one such child in my name welcomes me."

MATTHEW 18:1-5

Isn't it incredible? We spend much of our early lives anxious to grow up and become mature adults. We want to develop into people who are respected as knowledgeable and wise leaders or members of the community. Then, we have Jesus telling us that we are instead to become like children. He makes it clear that He doesn't want us to act childishly, but He wants us to be childlike in our faith and trust in Him. And above all, we need a humble and sincere heart. Since these traits are more easily found in children, children then become our model of behavior.

Personally, I didn't like where this passage was leading me. Of all the tasks God could give me, this one was probably the worst. I had prided myself on how far I had come as a respected businessperson in the community. I was a CPA, a board member of a well known local bank, on numerous boards of non-profit organizations—in short, something of a leader in the community. It seemed that God was now leading me backwards and I resisted this greatly.

Then something happened about twelve years ago that I will never forget for as long as I live. Halfway through an eighth grade CCD (Sunday school) class I was teaching, one of the boys angrily jumped out of his seat and, nearly shouting, demanded, "Why do I have to be here? What good is all this God stuff anyway? My parents don't go to church and we don't pray at home. I never see any of this stuff on TV or in magazines or newspapers. Nobody talks about it at home and I sure don't talk to my friends about this. It's illegal to talk about God at school and my parents don't need it at work, so why do I have to be here?" Just as suddenly, he sat down, with his arms folded, and his head down. All I could see in this young man was deep anger and frustration.

Well, I was about to read him the "party line" about why we need to go to church and obey the Commandments, but the words would not come out. The truth of his words left me speechless and, like the rest of us, guilty as charged.

I have replayed this scene over and over in my mind many times. I now know what that boy was talking about. He was begging me to prove to Him that there is a God. He couldn't see

Him at home, school, on the TV or anywhere else in his world experience. Like all of us, he needed to have something to hope for in the future. This boy wanted to know that his life would have a purpose more than he could see right then. He desperately wanted to believe in a God like the one I was describing each Sunday, but at this point in his young life, the story of God was just like many of the fairy tales he had heard growing up. He could find no outward proof of God anywhere in his world, so he couldn't help but conclude that it was just another fiction. For him, without the evidence, God just didn't exist.

I wish I could finish the story about this young man and tell you how he eventually came around and found a friendship with God. But I cannot. I don't know what happened to him. For all I know, he may someday find his way home since that has been and will always be my personal prayer for him. I don't even remember his name but I do remember his words, as we all should. I believe his words will echo through the heavens on that last day and many people will realize too late what we have done to God's children. Through our own lack of personal spiritual accountability, we actually deny them access to God. The example of our daily lives should lead people to God, not away from Him.

This event caused me to do some research about God and children. Read what Jesus said in these verses:

> *Jesus said to his disciples, "Occasions for stumbling are bound to come, but woe to anyone by whom they come! It would be better for you if a millstone were hung around your neck and you were thrown into the sea than for you to cause one of these little ones to stumble."*
>
> LUKE 17:1-2

The catechism reinforces this message to an even greater extent:

> Anyone who uses the power at his disposal in such a way that it leads others to do wrong becomes guilty of scandal and responsible for the evil that he has directly or indirectly encouraged. (CCC 2287)

To be clear, Jesus was not only referring to children as little ones but also to all who are young and vulnerable in their faith. Remember that we can cause others to sin not only by doing the wrong things but also by not doing the right things. Sins of omission and commission are equally deadly. Did you appreciate the weight of the words Christ used? This is the sweet baby Jesus from those manger scenes. It's the loving Christ that died for us on the cross. It's the same man that, as Scripture often says, had compassion on all those He encountered (Matthew 9:36) and all those He healed (Matthew 8:16). What is going on here?

The answer is simple. We are seeing deep into God's heart, as reflected in Christ's words. Someone once said to me, "Do you know why babies are so wonderfully cute and innocent? It's because they are gifts fresh from the hand of God." Children are God's gift to us. Listen to the key word in that sentence: "gift." When we abuse them, reject them, fail to teach them about God and hurt them in any way, we will someday have to answer directly to God. And make no mistake about it: His judgment in this area of sin will be most harsh.

I remember what my parish priest once told me concerning children and how they behave today. "When we were growing up," he'd say, "we knew the difference between right and wrong. We still chose to do the wrong stuff, but we also knew that if we ever got caught, we'd "catch it" from our parents. And as usual, we did get caught, and yes, we also received the punishment. Kids today still choose to do the wrong stuff from time to time. But, unlike us, they don't know the difference between right and wrong because they no longer know what is right and what is wrong. You might say that we as kids were immoral; but the kids of today are amoral— they are without morals."

I believe he was right. But where, then, does that put us as parents who are ultimately responsible for the training and spiritual upbringing of our children? How will God judge us on this matter?

If you don't like the above verses, then read the verses that are cross-referenced to Matthew 18:5-9. These related passages are no easier to comply with; in fact they only confirm what we already know to be true.

As you walk along on the Road to Grace, you are bound to see many children who will need your attention. How will you respond? How do you treat them now? Don't allow yourself to get caught on this issue. Children are much too important to God.

13

Bottom Line #6: Please Bring Them Home

Certain pieces of Scripture can cause great anxiety as well as passionate arguments amongst Christians.

I remember having discussions with friends about how harshly God treated the Israelites in the Old Testament. Even though they were God's chosen people, many of them lost their lives because they did not follow God's laws, even when their non-compliance was apparently due to seemingly simple or minor infractions. Then, my friends and I would say how thankful we were that the New Testament Jesus came along when He did, implying that Jesus "softened" the rules, thereby giving us more leeway to sin.

Yet as I read Christ's words of the Gospels, I hear not only love and compassion, but also an expectation of obedience and compliance with His laws not unlike God's expectations found in the Old Testament. Scripture reminds us that,

> *Jesus Christ is the same yesterday and today and forever.*
>
> HEBREWS 13:8

God has not changed. Don't be fooled by any perceived change of tone or emphasis from one book of the Bible to another. Satan would love for you to think that the rules have been eased up over the centuries. They have not been changed. Think of God as you would a diamond. Both have many facets or characteristics. Just because we choose to focus on the more pleasant sides such as God's love and mercy, it doesn't diminish the existence and importance of His other attributes such as justice and the demand for obedience. This is another prime reason for studying all the aspects of God's nature. In the end, as He said to Moses, He's the same God through all of time:

God said to Moses, "I AM WHO I AM."

EXODUS 3:14

So what's the message here? Again the answer is a simple one. God's ultimate concern is to get all of His children back home again:

And this is the will of him who sent me, that I should lose nothing of all that he has given me, but raise it up on the last day.

JOHN 6:39

God wants to bring us home because He knows the alternative—hell. And when you read this Scripture from God's perspective, that alternative comes clearly into view. I think that's the piece we are either missing or discounting from our narrow view of salvation. Many of us just refuse to believe in the existence of such a place.

We seem to be constantly focusing our attention on God's loving side. But as I said earlier, He does have other sides to His personality. We must never forget, for example, that He is a just and holy God as well. Consider this: If there is no hell, then why would we need a Savior? There would be nothing to save us from! Jesus' death on the cross proves the existence of hell. He would not have gone through all that horror for no reason. The horror of hell produced the horror of the cross.

Without hell, the whole story of Christianity would be vastly different. Hell presents an incredible threat to our eternal security, so God had to take drastic measures to save us—and this proves how much He truly loves us. He wants us all to be home with Him in heaven and He has taken the ultimate steps to prove this point.

Many of us have great difficulty understanding why God's rules seem so harsh and unyielding. But again, I believe it's because God has the ultimate view of what can happen to us. His eternal plan for us does exist, but to us it is either incomprehensible or parts of it have not yet been revealed. But in any event, the stakes are enormous and incalculable.

Christ gives us another look at how important He felt His ministry was to our spiritual survival in His words to Peter just before He returned to heaven. One of the last things Jesus ever said to Peter gives us the bottom line on all we've discussed so far. See how emphatic Christ was as He spoke to Peter, His right-hand man:

When they had finished breakfast, Jesus said to Simon Peter, "Simon son of John, do you love me more than these?" He said to him, "Yes, Lord; you know that I love you." Jesus said to him, "Feed my lambs." A second time he said to him, "Simon son of John, do you love me?" He said to him, "Yes, Lord; you know that I love you." Jesus said to him, "Tend my sheep." He said to him the third time, "Simon son of John, do you love me?" Peter felt hurt because he said to him the third time, "Do you love me?" And he said to him, "Lord, you know everything; you know that I love you." Jesus said to him, "Feed my sheep."

After this he said to him, "Follow me."

JOHN 21:15-17, 19

I cannot think of another place in the Bible where God or Jesus stated something three times to person. It was so important to Jesus that He made sure Peter and those nearby heard His heart's desire. It could even be argued that this was Christ's last personal request before He would return to heaven. What's the bottom line? Jesus came as close to pleading for something as He ever did. He was asking Peter (and us), to please take care of His precious children and to not let them go astray. He wants us to help bring them home to Him.

Once more, our charge is clear and Christ's need is unambiguous. We are to bring those around us, along with us, as we move toward Him on that Road to Grace. After all He did for us, let us not fail in this mission.

14

Bottom Line #7: What to do About Sin?

As I noted earlier, I struggled greatly with the question of sin all throughout my youth. A kind of tug of war was always going on in my mind regarding the official Catholic definitions of mortal sins and venial sins. Into the mix I would throw extenuating circumstances as I sought loopholes and mitigating factors in order to convince God and myself that I wasn't such a bad person after all.

While preparing to give a talk about healing prayer to a group of people, I came across two parallel stories in the New Testament concerning Jesus and how He dealt with sin in the lives of two specific people. I think both cases definitively show how He views sin in our lives as well. Read the first story:

Now in Jerusalem by the Sheep Gate there is a pool, called in Hebrew Beth-zatha, which has five porticoes. In these lay many invalids—blind, lame, and paralyzed. One man was there who had been ill for thirty-eight years. When Jesus saw him lying there and knew that he had been there a long time, he said to him, "Do you want to be made well?" The sick man answered him, "Sir, I have no one to put me into the pool when the water is stirred up; and while I am making my way, someone else steps down ahead of me."

Jesus said to him, "Stand up, take your mat and walk." At once the man was made well, and he took up his mat and began to walk.

Later Jesus found him in the temple and said to him, "See, you have been made well! Do not sin any more, so that nothing worse happens to you."

JOHN 5:2-9, 14

Now read the second:

Early in the morning he came again to the temple. All the people came to him and he sat down and began to teach them. The scribes and the Pharisees brought a woman who had been caught in adultery; and making her stand before all of them, they said to him, "Teacher, this woman was caught in the very act of committing adultery. Now in the law Moses commanded us to stone such women. Now what do you say?" They said this to test him, so that they might have some charge to bring against him. Jesus bent down and wrote with his finger on the ground. When they kept on questioning him, he straightened up and said to them, "Let anyone among you who is without sin be the first to throw a stone at her." And once again he bent down and wrote on the ground. When they heard it, they went away, one by one, beginning with the elders; and Jesus was left alone with the woman standing before him. Jesus straightened up and said to her, "Woman, where are they? Has no one condemned you?" She said, "No one, sir." And Jesus said, "Neither do I condemn you. Go your way, and from now on do not sin again."

JOHN 8: 2-11

These two unforgettable stories show us both Jesus' compassion and His expectation that the behavior of both people will change. The man by the pool received a physical healing that was a long time in coming. But to receive the spiritual healing he required, he needed to repent, that is, turn from his sinful behavior once and for all and seek God's forgiveness.

The woman caught in adultery was also rescued from certain death. In a sense, she was being healed before the people could hurt her. Christ held back the fury of the men who were ready to stone her. He taught both her and them a lesson none would soon forget.

Both people were in a bad place physically and spiritually. Jesus' solution was not only to heal them, but also to tell them plainly what they needed to do in their spiritual lives from that point forward. They were both in danger, but Jesus also saw that they both had a tendency to sin—a greater danger. And to be healed spiritually, they both had to do the same thing: repent and stop sinning. That's it, plain and simple. Just seek forgiveness from God and stop committing that sin.

Talk about bottom lines! He knew what each person was doing. He knew they had a weakness for their pet sins and that they cherished those sinful tendencies. That is the key word here: cherish. He was telling both people that as long as they continued to harbor and keep their sin, they were at great risk. Just like the prodigal son, they could lose everything, including their own salvation. How? Because when we choose sin, we are choosing the kind of life it offers over the life God offers. You can't have both; they are mutually exclusive. If you choose to sin, then you choose not to serve God. If you choose to continue to sin, then you have chosen to step off of the Road to Grace and are now committing yourself to another direction which will lead you away from God even if it's "temporary".

The longer we continue to take pleasure in a particular form of sinful behavior, the more likely it will become a treasured habit. These are harder habits to get rid of and they are more likely to completely destroy us. Jesus knew this. That's why He told the man at the pool as well as the adulterous woman to stop sinning. He knew them and knew they treasured their sinful habits.

Many people think that God can tolerate our sin until we get around to confessing it, if at all, but in truth He cannot. His nature cannot coexist with sin no more than fire and water can coexist. That's why Scripture tells us that sin separates us from God:

Rather, your iniquities have been barriers between you and your God, and your sins have hidden his face from you so that he does not hear.

ISAIAH 59:2

Clearly, sin not only builds a wall between God and us, but also pushes God away from us and eventually moves Him out of our lives. These verses have even more to say:

For those who live according to the flesh set their minds on the things of the flesh, but those who live according to the Spirit set their minds on the things of the Spirit. To set the mind on the flesh is death, but to set the mind on the Spirit is life and peace. For this reason the mind that is set on the flesh is hostile to God; it does not submit to God's law—indeed it cannot, and those who are in the flesh cannot please God.

But you are not in the flesh; you are in the Spirit, since the Spirit of God dwells in you. Anyone who does not have the Spirit of Christ does not belong to him.

ROMANS 8: 5-8, 9

Adulterers! Do you not know that friendship with the world is enmity with God? Therefore whoever wishes to be a friend of the world becomes an enemy of God.

JAMES 4:4

The catechism also weighs in heavily on this issue:

> You ask and do not receive, because you ask wrongly, to spend it on your passions (James 4:3). If we ask with a divided heart, we are "adulterers"; God cannot answer us, for He desires our well-being, our life. (CCC 2737)

When we harbor sin, any sinful desire, we are telling God that we cannot give up sin just yet. Maybe we promise to do so in the future but for now we cannot. The prodigal son must have also said the same things while he was away from his father. Remember, while he was indulging in his sins, he was at great risk and peril. Had he died in that state (essentially what Catholics consider the state of mortal sin), he would have lost everything, including his eternal life.

There is another piece of Scripture that helps put all of this into clear perspective. One of the criticisms of the Catholic faith is that the words "mortal sin" do not show up anywhere in Scripture. I wanted to find some mention of mortal sin or its clear equivalent in the Bible. I discovered that there is a sin described in the Bible that will never be forgiven by God. This is how Jesus describes it:

> *Therefore I tell you, people will be forgiven for every sin and blasphemy, but blasphemy against the Spirit will not be forgiven. Whoever speaks a word against the Son of Man will be forgiven, but whoever speaks against the Holy Spirit will not be forgiven, either in this age or in the age to come.*
>
> MATTHEW 12:31-32

The Gospel writer Mark describes what Jesus said this way:

> *...but whoever blasphemes against the Holy Spirit can never have forgiveness, but is guilty of an eternal sin.*
>
> MARK 3:29

But what does it mean to speak against or blaspheme the Holy Spirit? The unpardonable sin is committed when we refuse to acknowledge God's power and authority in Jesus Christ. We literally attribute that power to someone or something else—Satan, for example. When we do this, we have effectively shut ourselves off from God. Jesus said that these people cannot be forgiven not because their sins are so bad, but simply because they would never ask for forgiveness.

Why? Because they have sinned for so long and gone so far from God that they don't even know that they are lost. They cannot see that their actions are offensive to God. These make-believers are no longer even aware that what they do is considered sin and deeply offensive to God.

Here is another good reason for getting to know God intimately. How important is it to know when we have broken His law or made Him unhappy? It's eternally important. My disobedience here and now can actually affect my eternal disposition. That's what we learn about God as we read and understand His words in Scripture. Ignorance of the Law will not save us. Why? Because we have access to God's Law, now more than ever. We can no longer say that we didn't know we were breaking God's rules. The Internet and the explosion of the information age has taken that excuse away from us. God's words and instructions are readily available today. It is our job as Catholics to know God's word and to therefore know when we have offended Him.

Think of this situation in the following manner. When I begin to sin, it's like I'm taking a baby step away from God and beginning to put myself at risk. The more steps I take in that direction, the more sin I commit, the greater my risk and exposure. Before too long, I have walked so far away from Him that He no longer is in my sight or memory. Did He leave me? No, I left Him just as the prodigal son left his father. It doesn't mean that God forgets about me; He does not, He cannot forget about me. It does mean He will patiently wait for me to return, like the father in the story of the prodigal son. But it's up to me to make the choice to return to Him.

If I let the sin continue, I will probably no longer consider it a sin because I have been doing it for so long that it now feels normal and maybe even a natural part of my life. I therefore see no reason to return home and seek the protection of my Father. But still, He waits for me.

It's also possible that perhaps other people around me are doing the same things as I am, reinforcing the idea that the sin is normal behavior. When I was a young person downgrading serious sins to the status of venial sin, I did it so I wouldn't feel I had to confess them. I took "license" with God's word and gained a feeling of liberty to go on committing these kinds of sins because I decided that they weren't a big deal. I was literally telling the Holy Spirit that I was not guilty of any sin. But my ongoing sin represented my personal choice to continue to reject God's Spirit in the world, His most sacred Holy Spirit. My actions therefore, blasphemed or rejected God's Spirit. My heart had become hard and arrogant toward God. Accordingly, the commission of mortal sin results from a hardening of our hearts.

Consider this situation. Just picture the poor Catholic walking along the Road to Grace and encountering something that tempts him or her to step off the road and join in on some forbidden activity. When we let this happen, we cease our movement toward God. We become like the prodigal son because our desire is to leave the Father. We probably don't see it that way. We'll see it as just a mild diversion or innocent distraction for just a short while. It's no big deal since we never intended to permanently leave God. But in God's eyes it is a big deal. He will see it as our becoming involved in something unhealthy. Think about it. How many marriages and long-term relationships have been destroyed because of just one "minor" romantic encounter with another person? It's the same thing with God.

We may not have intended to go off the road or perhaps we thought that a little diversion would not be harmful. But as long as we stay with that diversion we stay away from God and the pursuit of the things of God. This is very dangerous territory, a place that could kill us both physically and spiritually. Leaving the Road to Grace is never permissible or wise. When we do, we, like the prodigal son, are at great risk. That's why it's so important to be close to Him in a personal way. When we are, it's easier to hear and understand His instructions.

But again, never forget the one fantastic feature about our Father. Through all of our offending ways, He is patient with us and longsuffering. He will even wait until the very last moment just before we take our last breath to acknowledge our sin, seek forgiveness and return to Him.

Do not wait until then. Do it now.

15

Bottom Line #8: The True Nature of Sin

Keeping in mind the consumerist idea discussed earlier let's discuss how we actually see sin. Because we seldom see rules and laws being strictly enforced in our society, we've become accustomed to the notion that God will act in a similar manner when He enforces His laws with us. We have acquired the general notion that since He's such a loving and gentle God, He'll relent and be lenient with us when He doles out punishment for our sins.

An experience a year or so ago taught me something about how I had been viewing my own sins. I was late for teaching a class at a local university. I had a forty-five minute ride to get to school and I was at least ten minutes late in getting started. At the first traffic light, a State Police Trooper pulled up behind me and began to follow me—so, I had to keep to the posted speed limits. I was fully expecting him to soon pull off onto another road but he didn't; he stayed right there behind me for most of the trip. Going forty or forty-five miles per hour was bad enough, but then we got into other speed zones and the limits dropped to thirty miles per hour and even lower. Have you ever tried to drive only going as fast as the posted speed limits? It was maddening!

We came through a school zone where the posted limit was fifteen miles per hour. By then, I felt like getting out of the car and walking; it would have been faster. As I continued, I became more and more agitated and angry. I had all kinds of good reasons for wanting to exceed the posted speed limits, chief of which was that I feared being late for class and that my students would disappear before I got there.

Besides, being a teacher at a university is an important thing, is it not? So, I should be able to stretch the rules a bit, shouldn't I? After all, everyone else does, don't they? My anger was growing not only at the Trooper following me but also at my bad luck at getting caught in this situation. I verbally started letting God know how I felt. And then suddenly something dawned on me. I saw what I was doing. I was getting angry because I wasn't in control and getting what I wanted. I wanted the option of breaking the speed limits if I thought my reason was good enough and this Trooper was taking that option away from me.

I also saw this to be a good analogy as to how we break God's laws, changing or suspending the rules to fit our own needs whenever we want. As soon as I realized what was happening, I started to laugh out loud at how God works at showing us the truth in our lives. Just then, that State Trooper turned off onto another road. At that point, I prayerfully asked God to help get me to school on time and turned the whole thing over to Him. I had learned the lesson He wanted me to learn.

In our culture today, we think that freedom means that we can do pretty much whatever we want, whenever we feel like it as long as no one in our estimation gets hurt. But in reality, we have the freedom to do the things we want within pre-determined boundaries. God's laws have set those boundaries up for us, not just spiritually but also physically. They are there for our own protection. We rarely consider all the times that God has healed us or saved us from certain harm or destruction because we exceeded those boundaries. It's hard to see this because these events never transpire. God protects us even when we break His laws. But did you ever wonder what might have happened if He was not there to protect you? Read what Jesus said about how deadly sin can be:

> *If your right eye causes you to sin, tear it out and throw it away; it is better for you to lose one of your members than for your whole body to be thrown into hell. And if your right hand causes you to sin, cut it off and throw it away; it is better for you to lose one of your members than for your whole body to go into hell.*
>
> MATTHEW 5:29-30

Even though Jesus is speaking figuratively here, His examples are designed to be extreme so we can become convinced of how important it is to rid ourselves of any sinful habits that, left unchecked, could eventually hurt us not only physically but also for all eternity. It is better to endure the pain associated with the removal of our bad habit than to be subject to eternal damnation.

In my case, I wanted to exceed the speed limits because I felt my needs justified it. If this habit was left unchecked, it could very well destroy me, anyone else in my car at the time and others on the road. We do the same thing with regard to God's laws. Yet in truth, no one has the right to trump a law or directive from God.

The icing on the cake was that I arrived at class with ten whole minutes to spare! I don't know how He did it, but God is so good!

Finally, think of sin as being like a cancer in the body. It usually begins with just one small spot on the bone or in the tissue. But what happens? It can grow, and, unless it is stopped early, it will destroy the entire body. This is the true nature of sin. It breeds death, and it ultimately destroys the body.

The bottom line is that all sin is offensive to God. It really makes no difference whether it's venial or mortal in nature. The longer we allow sin to get a foothold in our life, the more likely it'll consume us like a cancerous disease. As Jesus said to all of us, "Stop sinning or something worse may happen to you!"

16

Bottom Line #9: Praying in the Lap of God

The biggest surprise I had concerning the topic of prayer occurred at the most fundamental level of my former understanding of it. The revelation unfolded before me in four distinct parts. Haddon Robinson, a distinguished professor at Gordon-Conwell Theological Seminary, explained prayer at its most basic level in the following way:

"I used to play a game with my two children when they were young. I would clutch some pennies in my hand and allow them to pry open my fingers to get the coins. My children would sit on my lap and work feverishly to get the money. Once they captured the coins, they would scream with delight and jump down to treasure their prize. I loved having my youngsters laugh and play while sitting on my lap. The pennies were insignificant." [1]

Suppose God's ultimate desire is to see us come to Him and ask for the things we need, not because it is orderly or respectful but simply because He loves to have us "on His lap?" Suppose He made us in such a way that in order to have the things we want and need, we would have to come to Him? In that case, we would want to be near Him as much as He wants to be near us—

and prayer is His way to bring us closer to Him.

Perhaps this is not too surprising a proposal for you. But I don't think anything surprised me more. I knew that prayer was a way to communicate with God. But this was a complete reversal. I now saw God as someone who wanted to be near me; In a sense, He needed me. In the past, I could not conceive of a God who would long to be near me and who would engineer things in my life, in such a way, as to draw me closer to Him.

When I encountered this idea for the first time, it saddened me greatly. It was like finding out that the one special person who you thought had little interest in you had instead been longing for your company for many years. Worse yet, I began to realize that in all the times I went to Him asking and pleading for things, I never once thought that all He wanted in return was, in a sense, to have me sit on His lap like a little boy and just press in close to Him. I felt like I had abused God and had taken advantage of His love and generosity for many years. I cannot put into words how devastated I was at this time. The following verse show's God's desire to be with us:

Listen! I am standing at the door, knocking; if you hear my voice and open the door, I will come in to you and eat with you, and you with me.

REVELATION 3:20

Again, these words bring us back to John 17 where Jesus is asking His Father not only to protect us after He returns to heaven but He also specifies that He wants us to be with Him for all time.

The image of Jesus personally knocking on our door is a strange one. Not only does He want to see us, but He wants to dine with us. Dining was a very special event in those days. It was an important sign of friendship and camaraderie. The main meal was the centerpiece of each day and who you spent it with had significance.

Yet this revelation made even more sense to me once I started putting it together with some of the key Scriptures we've been talking about. For example, look at the verses about the vine in John 15. They fit right into what we're discussing here. Or remember the two Great Commandments. Again, it's all about love. The next time you pray, imagine yourself going to God like a little child would and climbing up into His lap. Then picture yourself resting and leaning on Him. You're safe, secure and loved. Now start talking with Him.

17

Bottom Line #10: *Ora Labora*

I've struggled with prayer all my life. I didn't necessarily find it difficult to do, but it was boring and frequently didn't yield the results I wanted. So it wasn't on the top of my list of favorite things to do.

But real prayer is tough business—and realizing that real prayer is real work opened my eyes. Sometimes I still catch myself just "saying my prayers" and I have to stop and backup. I no longer believe in mechanically rattling off a string of Our Fathers or Hail Marys. Now as I pray, I actually imagine myself sitting on Gods lap like a small boy, talking to my Father about the things that trouble me (see Matthew 18:1-5 and also 2 Peter 2:2).

When I do this, I find it impossible to rattle anything off without really focusing and concentrating on giving my prayers real meaning. I'm too close to Him to be that disrespectful. But I am also learning to listen at the same time. I never want to go to Him and just ask anymore. I also want to know how I can help Him!

Believe it or not, God also has needs. He needs us to be His hands and feet here in this world. So my time in prayer is now more of a dialogue between us. But I have to be very careful. Jesus makes it quite clear how He expects me to do what He says:

Why do you call me "Lord, Lord," and do not do what I tell you?
LUKE 6:46

This verse echoes the crucial verses of Matthew 7:21-29 in which Jesus says clearly that only those who do the will of His Father will enter the Kingdom of God. His meaning is very straightforward: Don't bother going to God with your problems and needs if you only intend to follow His instructions partially or maybe not follow them at all. God doesn't work like a democracy.

He's more like a stern but benevolent Father dealing with His children. He has expectations for each of us and a clear set of rules for us to follow. He'll bless us with more than we can imagine, but He also expects us to listen to Him. I had always felt that prayer was something a person should do just before they went into a difficult situation, like an exam in school. Then I read a magazine article which suggested that Jesus treated prayer as *the chief work* of His own ministry on earth. For Him, the battle was the actual praying itself.

Think about how frequently in the Gospels Christ went off to pray for long periods of time. Remember especially the Garden of Gethsemane, where He struggled mightily with what He had to do:

In his anguish he prayed more earnestly, and his sweat became like great drops of blood falling down on the ground.
LUKE 22:44

Once He finished praying that night, Jesus was able to then walk confidently to the cross. He came through His crisis because He prepared for it by working at prayer. Every time He came back from praying He was able to continue His marvelous works and deeds. This was because of His relationship with His Father.

They were as one (see John 17:20-21) and prayer was the "glue" that kept them linked, the umbilical cord from God that supplied Him with all that He needed.

This then, should be our model. But it will require a great shift in our thinking. Prayer needs to go from being almost an afterthought action to the very first place we put our greatest efforts. In Latin the term is *Ora Labora.* Saint Benedict came up with this idea in the sixth century: "The prayer is the work and the work is the prayer.

I'm willing to bet that this little-known fact is what so many of us have overlooked for so many years. Can you imagine what would happen to our ministerial work and programs if we as Catholics and Christians put most of our efforts into prayer first and throughout the project? We would need seatbelts!

18

Bottom Line #11: Pray Without Ceasing

Early on in my walk with God, it was very difficult to remember to pray often. So I purchased a watch with an alarm that chimed on the hour. When it rang, I would stop and pray. It would ring during all kinds of situations. If it rang while I was on the phone, I would start to pray silently for the person I was talking with. It would also ring when I was upset with something or someone, prompting me to change my thought patterns.

Not only did it work incredibly well for my work at prayer, it had another interesting benefit. When people near me heard the alarm go off, they asked whether it was to remind me to take my medication. That gave me a chance to explain why I had set up the hourly alarm and to talk to them about praying frequently. So something I did to make my private time with God more fruitful became an opportunity to share God with others.

Pretty soon I no longer needed the watch to remind me. I had the habit and furthermore, I actually looked forward to my time with Him. Now we have something more like a constant dialogue, like you'd expect to have happen when you are driving or walking for a distance with a friend.

One of the shortest and most profound verses in the Bible speaks about this kind of prayer. It is telling us to do something that does not come easily for many of us:

...pray without ceasing...

1 THESSALONIANS 5:17

This is how we should be with God: Praying constantly as we work and play. He truly loves and encourages our prayers. Another important verse instructs,

We destroy arguments and every proud obstacle raised up against the knowledge of God, and we take every thought captive to obey Christ.

2 CORINTHIANS 10:4-5

If my thoughts are about a good thing or event, I give thanks to God. However when my thoughts are stressful and unpleasant because of problems I'm encountering, I prayerfully work on finding ways to solve these problems with God's help. On many occasions, I've found that I have to simply turn the whole matter or problem over to Him because it is well beyond my ability to deal effectively with it. In this way, I've been able to work at "taking every thought captive."

Whenever you have a thought about an upcoming event or problem, convert that concern into the form of a prayer. Instead of worrying or getting angry about it, pray a short prayer to God for His help. Pretty soon you'll see many of your thoughts taking on a more positive and productive role. Most important of all is that you will be putting what you believe about God into action in your own life.

Think of it this way. If Christ was visible and present in your life and He went with you everywhere you went, wouldn't you be asking for His advice and help from time to time? Well, just because He's not visible to you shouldn't change the situation. Pray all the time. In other words, talk to Him as if He was physically there with you. It does work, but it takes time and practice. Be patient—it's worth the effort.

19

Bottom Line #12: Interceding for Others

The fourth part of my prayer revelation was intercession, a type of prayer where we can go before God and speak to Him on behalf of others and their needs. After experiencing the first revelation of depending totally on God, the second revelation of treating prayer as the chief work and then the concept of praying without ceasing, I was now ready to intercede for others.

The idea behind intercession is that we can now go before Him as His precious child and request whatever we need as well as for the needs of others. He said to us:

Ask, and it will be given you; search, and you will find; knock, and the door will be opened for you. For everyone who asks receives, and everyone who searches finds, and for everyone who knocks, the door will be opened.

MATTHEW 7:7-8

Many people have a difficult time understanding these two verses. They especially get confused about the idea of asking for anything and expecting that they'll receive it. Just as you will not let your children have access to something you know is bad for them, neither will God grant requests that He knows will end up hurting you. When your own children are young and innocently ask you for good things, isn't it very hard to refuse them? It's the same with God. We are His children.

Whenever you are in a right relationship with God, He will give you your heart's desires. Why? Because by definition, if you are that close to Him, His will becomes your will. You will automatically seek the things He wants. Your prayer requests for yourself and others will automatically become good things for you to have because your desires and God's desires are one and the same. Your prayers will be answered.

Here's another good reason for getting closer to God. Your prayers will be answered more frequently and easily. Read what the catechism says about this:

> Once committed to conversion, the heart learns to pray in faith. Faith is a filial adherence to God beyond what we feel and understand. It is possible because the beloved Son gives us access to the Father. He can ask us to "seek" and to "knock," since he himself is the door and the way. (CCC 2609)

Jesus is the doorway to heaven. Don't be afraid to ask. Incidentally, this is how healing prayers work as well. Once you link up with God, all kinds of great miracles become possible and even more probable in their occurrence.

> *All things can be done for the one who believes.*
>
> MARK 9:23

I was in a steakhouse in Atlanta with a group of friends a few years ago. We were all businessmen in town for a conference. Our waiter, a young college student named Eric, came to the table to take our drink order. Just before Eric was about to leave and get our drinks, one of the men at our table, without any warning, said to Eric, "We're about to say grace before dinner.

Would you like us to pray for you or for anyone else you know of who needs prayer?"

Well, I almost fell out of my chair. Even though this was Atlanta, part of the "Bible Belt," one rarely saw this kind of thing in restaurants there. But much to Eric's credit, after a brief hesitation, he replied yes, there was someone to pray for. He didn't ask for himself, but for his friend Mike who had just broken his leg and lost his job. So we all prayed.

Now, let me tell you what happened. If Eric came back to our table once that night he was there at least twenty-five times. He just couldn't do enough for us. And at the end of the meal, he wanted to know more about us and why we prayed that way. Most importantly, he wanted to know more about Jesus Christ. My friend, who first asked Eric the question, took a chance and it paid off. He taught me that if I want to be a real Christian and Catholic, I have to be ready to take a risk if I hear God telling me to do something. It was a very practical lesson. Now you tell me—was God happy that evening or not? Prayer is the work, and the work is the prayer.

But some of you reading this probably still do not believe me. Would you like more proof? Well, this story isn't over yet. Later on that evening, one of the other men in our group told us that before we all went out to eat that night, he prayed that one of us, or maybe all of us, during the course of that evening would be able to share Christ with someone who didn't know Him. God answered that prayer, in that restaurant. We were all able to intercede for Mike and ask God to help him. Is that awesome or what? *Ora Labora!*

Many other dramatic events have occurred in my prayer life. The answers to my prayers have actually proven to me, beyond a shadow of a doubt, that God is real. He does hear our requests and He does answer them. Fortunately, someone gave me a wonderful idea early on in my walk with God. He suggested the use of a prayer journal where each prayer request could be recorded on a single page. He said to record only the major prayer requests in this journal, with the date and some detail about the reasons for each prayer. He also said to ask God specifically for what was needed. Detail about the request was important. Then I was to pray until an answer came back. When the prayer was answered, I was to date it in the journal and describe God's response in detail.

I am amazed whenever I go back over my prayer journal and see God's footprints in my life. In this little book, I have what amounts to a scrapbook of the moments God entered my life and saved, helped and loved not only me but also those I asked Him to touch. This is my own real personal proof that God exists. It has convinced me beyond a doubt of His presence. People may ask why I've written this book. They may even question my credentials or my authority to say these things. All I have to do is to show them my prayer journal. Between its covers is overwhelming evidence of God's presence in my life. He has saved me and others around me on numerous occasions. That's the bottom line and the best reason in the world for me to want to tell others about Him.

You must also remember that I've been trained all my adult life to be a critical and skeptical auditor and accountant. Despite that influence (and maybe even because of that training), I feel the evidence is overwhelming and must be reported. He is real; He does exist and it's time we all realize this truth.

Later, God did something else to prove to me even more that He is with us. He brought me into the wonderful world of healing prayer. Saint Paul's letter to the Ephesians tells us:

Therefore be imitators of God, as beloved children, and live in love, as Christ loved us and gave himself up for us, a fragrant offering and sacrifice to God.

EPHESIANS 5:1-2

Paul advises us to be like God and to act like Christ to others around us. This always sounded to me like an impossible task, but I nevertheless tried to understand exactly what Jesus did for people while He was here on earth. I reasoned that if I studied His actions and thoughts, then I would have a good model to follow.

Christ dealt with people in basically five different ways. He listened, loved, healed, taught and prayed with everyone that He encountered. Those five verbs encapsulate His example for us to imitate. Recall John's Gospel, when Jesus meets the man by the pool at Bethesda and the woman caught in adultery. These are two good examples of how God heals. But Jesus makes the most interesting point with the man at the pool.

The Scriptures tell us that the man had been lying there crippled, for thirty-eight years.

When Jesus saw him lying there and knew that he had been there a long time, he said to him, "Do you want to be made well?"

JOHN 5:6

The question Jesus asks him is curious. He knew the man was lame for all those years, so why should He ask this question? Wouldn't anyone in that situation want to be healed? But Jesus knows what is in the heart of man and He asked this question for a good reason. When someone is sick for so long, that sickness can become a way of life for him or her. He may think that there can never be any help or rescue from the situation, so they fall into a sort of chasm, where there is little or no hope for the future. Christ was really asking him if, should he be healed, he would change his attitudes and live his life in accordance with God's laws or merely return to his old ways.

The big question is not whether a person will be healed but what they will do with the extra time they receive to live after

God heals them. That's what Jesus was asking this crippled man. God always knows the exact extent of the healing we need. Some healings only extend a person's life for a matter of weeks or even days. But that can be just enough time for them to repair relationships or to come back to the Lord. In other cases the healing can go on for months or years.

Additionally, there have been many cases where people were not healed physically on the outside but instead received a healing inside on an emotional, psychological and/or spiritual level. God knows what we need the most and He'll give it to us if we're willing to accept it and change our ways. Even when Jesus miraculously fed the five thousand people (see Matthew 14:13-21), they all were hungry again the next morning. For that matter, everyone that Jesus ever healed did eventually die. So, the bottom line about healing prayer is not the healing. It's what you do once you are healed.

Will you go back to the same old lifestyle or will you find a new home on God's lap? Are you willing to be born again? Are you willing to be healed, to that degree? If so, what will you do with your new life, regardless of how much more time God grants you? It's something to really think about.

I know from my own experience with healing prayer that it does work. Why? Because I know there is a Holy Spirit that will come to us and that has the power to heal. We who believe in that power understand that we are only mere vessels through which God's healing grace can flow. Many people misunderstand this point. No one heals except Jesus Christ, through His Holy Spirit. We are merely "channels," for God's healing power.

There are a few more things about prayer that you should know. One of the main reasons why so many of us may not pray frequently is that we think that our problems involve people and forces that we cannot imagine having any control over. Maybe we feel so inadequate and helpless that we don't even know how to ask for help. Or perhaps the problems seem so large and frightful that we give up asking. But remember the words of Saint Paul:

For our struggle is not against enemies of blood and flesh, but against the rulers, against the authorities, against the cosmic powers of this present darkness, against the spiritual forces of evil in the heavenly places.

EPHESIANS 6:12

In other words, Satan. We need to pray frequently for God's protection and help no matter how impossible that challenge may be. Our battle is with spiritual forces whose supernatural capabilities far exceed ours. Without God we are totally unprotected against this kind of threat. Consider the early church and why it was so successful. This early church (our own Catholic Church) grew, became powerful and touched many lives despite the religious persecution of the day because,

They devoted themselves to the apostles' teaching and fellowship, to the breaking of bread and the prayers.

ACTS 2:42

Notice the last three words: these were *the key* to their success. Remember, practice praying without ceasing. And finally,

- If we study the Word of God in the Bible without praying, then all we have become is theological Pharisees.
- If we have church functions and gatherings without prayer, then all we have are great parties.
- If we go to Confession, receive Communion and attend Mass regularly, all without prayer, then all we have are rituals.
- When we prayerfully study the Bible and God's word and we do it in His presence, the doors and windows to our hearts

and souls will open and He will feed us.
• When we gather with others, we have an opportunity to reach out and help them. We can then hear what they need directly from them. We can continue to pray with them and for them long after those gatherings. Never, ever discount the power of praying with someone, softly out loud and in front of him or her. It is a very powerful tool. Let them quietly hear your heart petitions on their behalf as you go before the throne of God. It's so effective and so personal.
• When we engage Christ in the Sacraments, our homage to Him reaches into the deepest parts of heaven and it creates the most pleasing aroma to God and is music to His ears.

As you can see, the changes in my spiritual life have been dramatic and very different from my upbringing as a Catholic. However, the fortunate thing is that a sturdy foundation and vessel was already there to receive these revelations. Those teachers I had in grammar and high school crafted it. As I look back now, I am eternally grateful to those precious people but I do wonder if our children today are being given a similar base on which they can build a faith. We'll talk more about this in the following chapters.

20

Bottom Line #13: How We are to Treat Others

How can other Catholics come to a knowledge and experience of God similar to my own? This is my main concern.

In the northeastern United States, where I live, many of our church experiences seem more like memorial services rather than active living interactions with God Himself and others in the congregation. I don't fault the clergy for this. I blame us, the people. I shouldn't even call it blame; it's more like a deep sadness caused by a lost opportunity.

We have the privilege of experiencing the Sacraments, coming into communion with the Lord and one another, but we seem to squander many of the opportunities. We could have so much more than what we have now with God. It's as if we are satisfied with dried crackers while God is offering us steak, lobster and other rich and wonderful faith foods.

We profess to believe in God but for some reason do not believe that He wants to be close or involved with us. Catholics, as a group, have created and accepted a sense of distance between themselves and God. We are reluctant to get too close and familiar with Him.

At a Mass I attended not long ago, I had a very strong sense of His presence. But do you know where I felt that God was standing? He wasn't up on the altar. Instead, He was waiting just inside the main doors to the church for each of us as we were leaving. I stood back and watched and listened to the conversations. As the Mass was concluding, people started to leave and I could almost hear Him audibly asking each person if He could accompany them home.

What a sad feeling I had. I don't think anyone realizes that this is the greatest gift we receive from the Mass. When we receive Communion, we literally receive Christ. We as Catholics believe that He is physically present in the Host that we consume. We therefore can take Jesus home with us and to wherever we go throughout the week.

But we need to acknowledge Him and His presence—and see Him as being a real person. At the risk of sounding silly, think of it this way. Suppose you went to an event and found out that Superman was a real person after all. And then suppose he came up to you and offered to do anything you'd like or need over the course of the next week? Can you imagine going through the following week and never asking him to help you? Now that would be insane!

Well, in a similar way that's what many of us do with Jesus who can do so much more than any super person. We leave Mass and hardly think about Him during the week. That is insane.

My spiritual life always receives a boost whenever I find myself working and worshipping with others who truly believe in Jesus Christ and His real presence. Christianity is at its best when experienced in groups. It's like love. It doesn't work well if there's no one to direct your love toward.

At times I have felt very alone in this walk with the Lord. If I speak of my relationship with Him, even at Bible studies at times, it's amazing how many people really do not know what I'm talking about. We hear about our Christian brothers and sisters in other denominations developing personal relationships with God and many of us wonder what that's all about. But it's very similar to what's being described here on these pages. We need to develop a practical walking faith with God. We need to move and act on this faith, applying it to issues we encounter. Then it will effectively serve us and direct us as we move through our daily routines.

More importantly, we need to be aware of God's presence so that when we come upon a situation where we need Him, or better yet, when we can be of help to Him, we will go to Him and we will hear what He has to tell us. God does come to each of us in many different ways and the key question is always whether and how we will respond to Him. Yet we don't talk about these things with one another. At best we'll listen to a sermon or homily on Sunday and maybe even a taped message from some priest or minister.

But how often have you sat down with anyone and really discussed what you thought about God? We may get snippets and glimpses of how people think and that's it. By way of example, let me tell you about something that happened to me a year or so ago.

I received a phone call from the teacher of the Confirmation class in our church. She was frustrated in trying to get her class ready for Confirmation. The students just did not seem to understand the seriousness of the Sacrament they were about to receive. Out of desperation, she required them to come to the Bible study class I was holding at the time. She called late the same day of our class to let me know they were coming. I was panicked because approximately twenty or so teenagers might show up and I had nothing prepared to teach them! So my wife and I prayed about it and turned it over to God, trusting Him to take care of the preparation needs. Then we went to the Bible study.

We got there early and set up several large rectangular tables end to end. The regular Bible study group (who had no idea we were having guests) started showing up and for some reason, they all sat on one side of the tables. When the students came in, they sat on the opposite side of the tables and just stared at the grownups across from them. I looked at my wife, swallowed hard and opened the meeting in prayer. And then God took over.

One of the older members of our Bible group immediately started talking to the kids. He began telling them about how important Jesus was to him. Then another lady also gave the same kind of a story. The students asked more and more questions and before I knew it, God was moving in the lives of these people on both sides of the table.

I realized that probably for the first time in their lives, these kids heard another Catholic grownup, who wasn't a member of the clergy, explain in their own words what God meant to them. And for all I know, perhaps this was the first time these older folks ever shared their personal feelings about God with anyone they didn't really know. I leaned over to my wife as this was happening and whispered, "Please tell me that it can't be this simple!"

It is that simple! Yet for some reason, we as Catholics just have a hard time telling others what we believe about our faith. Those teenagers and the members of the Bible study group left the room that night with something priceless. We shared the good news of salvation with our children. We expressed our faith in God out loud! It may not have been easy for us but it was necessary and we did it. Once again, if we agree that God is the most important factor in our lives, then we must also agree that stepping onto a path that leads to Him is of prime importance as well. But while many or even most of us will agree on this point, we allow other things in our life to prevent us from embarking on the Road to Grace. This has to change. Too much is at stake.

Consider the following questions and answers:

Question: What's the definition of insanity?

Answer: Continuing to do things the same way as usual and expecting the results to be different.

Now take it one step further.

Question: What's the definition of eternal insanity?

Answer: Continuing to largely ignore God every day and expecting Him to welcome us into heaven on that last day.

My point here is simple. If we continue to ignore the fact that we are to export the Good News of Jesus Christ to others, then nothing will change and in the end we will lose everything. But we cannot export it until we have imported Christ into our lives. Similarly, the status quo with our children who do not know God will not change, until we change first.

Sometimes it seems that following Him will never get easier and people will never really want to start looking for Him. I thought that after the attacks of September 11, 2001 more Catholics would genuinely start to seek Him. But the surge in church attendance soon after that tragedy, slackened off after just a few months. It's as if someone threw a big rock in the pond of life making large waves that knocked many of us off our comfortable "lily pads." After a while, though, the ripples subsided and everyone returned to business as usual. It's time to change our approach to God.

I've had a daily, running conversation with God about what He expects of us and how we are to treat others. Our discussion always returns me to a few very telling Scriptures:

Everyone therefore who acknowledges me before others, I also will acknowledge before my Father in heaven; but whoever denies me before others, I also will deny before my Father in heaven.

MATTHEW 10:32-33

So when you are offering your gift at the altar, if you remember that your brother or sister has something against you, leave your gift there before the altar and go; first be reconciled to your brother or sister, and then come and offer your gift.

MATTHEW 5:23-24

For if you forgive others their trespasses, your heavenly Father will also forgive you; but if you do not forgive others, neither will your Father forgive your trespasses.

MATTHEW 6:14-15

What did you read in these verses? Did you feel the two Great Commandments coming through again? They really do sum up all of God's law. They are the greatest Bottom Lines of all. The catechism also explains quite well how Jesus sees these kinds of commands as being pivotal and in a person's conversion:

From the Sermon on the Mount onwards, Jesus insists on "conversion of heart": reconciliation with one's brother before presenting an offering on the altar, love of enemies, and prayer for persecutors, prayer to the Father in secret, not heaping up empty phrases, prayerful forgiveness from the depths of the heart, purity of heart, and seeking the Kingdom before all else. This filial conversion is entirely directed to the Father.

(CCC 2608, emphasis added).

No matter how you look at it, without love for God, for one another and for ourselves, everything we do for Him is wasted and fruitless. Furthermore, God will treat us in the same way we treat others. Do you remember the "Golden Rule?"

Do to others as you would have them do to you.

LUKE 6:31

Could it be any simpler? Then why can't we comply with these verses? We'll discuss the answer to this question and other related issues in a later chapter.

But for now let's continue to concentrate on building up the foundation Christ wants each of us to have in our lives. The mortar of that foundation is love, love in all that we do. Think about the absolute truth of Saint Paul's words in the "love chapter" of 1 Corinthians. We've all heard this famous section of Scripture, especially at weddings. But now read these words as found in a popular modern-day text, in the hope that they will have a greater impact and clearer meaning. Please, read this slowly… let it soak in.

If I speak with human eloquence and angelic ecstasy but don't love, I'm nothing but the creaking of a rusty gate.

If I speak God's Word with power, revealing all his mysteries and making everything plain as day, and if I have faith that says to a mountain, "Jump," and it jumps, but I don't love, I'm nothing.

If I give everything I own to the poor and even go to the stake to be burned as a martyr, but I don't love, I've gotten nowhere.

So, no matter what I say, what I believe, and what I do, I'm bankrupt without love.

Love never gives up.
Love cares more for others than for self.
Love doesn't want what it doesn't have.
Love doesn't strut,
Doesn't have a swelled head,
Doesn't force itself on others,
Isn't always 'me first,'
Doesn't fly off the handle,
Doesn't keep score of the sins of others,
Doesn't revel when others grovel,
Takes pleasure in the flowering of truth,

Puts up with anything,
Trusts God always,
Always looks for the best,
Never looks back,
But keeps going to the end.

1 CORINTHIANS 13:1-7, *The Message*

Can you imagine doing all of these things, yet having them all be worthless in God's eyes because there was no love motivating you? Moving a mountain by sheer faith (See Matthew 17:20) or offering yourself as a martyr would all be useless efforts simply because you did it all without the kind of love God requires and expects of us?

Recall our earlier discussion of Matthew 7:21-23: Jesus says He will not acknowledge certain people who claim to know Him. Even though they did great works of prophesying in God's name, driving out demons and other marvelous things, God will not recognize them because they did not do the will of His Father in heaven. And the will of the Father is that we should love God and one another.

It's the same thing with the love chapter of 1 Corinthians. This is a major bottom line from God, totally in sync with His most fundamental commands. This is what it all comes down to. As Catholics, we are called to invest ourselves in God, others and ourselves. Whatever we do to benefit ourselves and those closest to us, we are to do likewise for strangers. There is no difference between these groups of people. In God's eyes, we are all His children. Remember when the people in the crowds that followed Christ, told Jesus that His mother and brothers were looking for Him? How did He respond?

"Who is my mother, and who are my brothers?" And pointing to his disciples, he said, "Here are my mother and my brothers! For

whoever does the will of my Father in heaven is my brother and sister and mother."

MATTHEW 12:48-50

Until we understand and believe in these words, we are all just wasting our time as Christians and as Catholics. We are make-believers.

God is looking for those who want to invest themselves in their brothers and sisters. But make no mistake about it. He first needs us to invest ourselves in Him. He is seeking people who will help Him gather up His sheep so they can find their way home to Him. And if we tackle this task without first joining with Him, as He describes in John 15:1-17, we'll fail even as we begin. Is He calling you? Has He been calling you? Do you believe you are one of His children or not? Or are you too busy, frightened or embarrassed to respond?

Remember, God is the gatekeeper. He will ultimately judge and decide who gains eternal life. But don't let that fact be your motivation. Instead, let's go to Him because of who He is, what He's done for us and the fact that He loves us so much. Sometimes it's not easy to serve Him but He is easy to love.

The next chapter begins to talk about some of the things we'll encounter in trying to serve our God. As Jesus tells us in Matthew 28:19, where He lays out The Great Commission, He needs us. God actually needs us, now more than ever.

PART III

CHALLENGES TO OUR FAITH WALK

21

The Barriers to Living Out Our Faith: A Personal Testimony

True faith is not a spectator sport. Studying the Word, listening to wonderful conversations between Catholic theologians and clergy, hearing a homily at Mass are all good ways to help you develop in your walk with God. But if you claim to be a Catholic, you have to do the things revealed to us in the Scriptures, as well as in the catechism. In other words, we have to live out our faith every moment of every day in the most common and routine events we encounter.

Catholicism is a verb. I found out that no matter what I said, it always seems to come down to what I do. That's what people see. Just as the eighth grader in CCD class noted, if there's no physical evidence of grownups doing what God says, then there really mustn't be a God. People look to us to be examples of how we should live. And it is right that they do this.

We Catholics are Christians! That means we are followers of Jesus Christ. That also means we agree with what Jesus says and what is clearly stated in the Bible. Consequently, we should be living our lives differently than other people in the world. After all, we're the ones that go to church every week. And again, we go there presumably because we believe in the founder of our church, Jesus Christ. This does not make us better than anyone else, it should make our behavior different. For example, I remember driving on a major highway one day and the traffic was quite heavy. Along comes a black Toyota Camry with one of those little fish symbols (a sign of Christianity) on the trunk lid. The lady driving was weaving in and out through the traffic at a high rate of speed. She was endangering her life and those around her. What did that action say to everyone who noticed the fish symbol? Remember, we are God's agents. We are His ambassadors.

So we are ambassadors for Christ, since God is making his appeal through us; we entreat you on behalf of Christ, be reconciled to God.

2 CORINTHIANS 5:20

If you give this piece of scripture some serious thought, it becomes evident that our job as Catholics is very important. We represent God's position on many of life's issues. If we are cavalier or not serious enough about our faith, we will misrepresent God to others and the consequences of that will always be very serious.

When I came to realize this point, it was very sobering. If my belief in God is truly important to me, then I have the same charge as a member of a religious order. I am to represent God to others by what I say and do.

But you are a chosen race, a royal priesthood, a holy nation, God's own people, in order that you may proclaim the mighty acts of him who called you out of darkness into his marvelous light.

1 PETER 2:9

It became obvious to me that going to Mass on Sundays was only a small part of what God expects of me. Developing a personal walking faith with God means a lot more than just learning about God's words or visiting a church. I had to start doing what He said, out where it counted, in the real world. Any other course of action would have been hypocritical. By not acting for Christ would guarantee that I would remain a make-believer for my entire life. So I chose to try to become a living example of His words.

I had discovered something in God's laws and personal presence that could make a big difference in how I approached my work, clients, friends and family. I wanted desperately to see these beliefs work well in my life. The catechism may surprise some of you who might think that only the clergy are responsible for acting as the "priests" of our Church. It sums this discussion up very thoroughly.

Christ, high priest and unique mediator, has made of the Church "a kingdom, priests for his God and Father." The whole community of believers is, as such, priestly. The faithful exercise their baptismal priesthood through their participation, each according to his own vocation, in Christ's mission as priest, prophet, and king. Through the sacraments of Baptism and Confirmation the faithful are "consecrated to be...a holy priesthood." (CCC 1546)

But these concepts are not easy to realize in the real world. There are many barriers or obstacles that can prevent us from being good, living examples of God's love and His desire to see us succeed.

This brings us to several very important questions. How do we physically follow Christ to the point where we can be a good representative of His laws and love? Is it something like a twelve-step program? How do we successfully comply with His laws and rules while living our daily lives? Is it really possible to do this? Or do we have to give up everything we own or shut ourselves off from society in order to accomplish what He wants? The short answer to all of these questions is yes, we can follow Him while living normal lives, working normal jobs and having friends and family. And no, we don't necessarily have to give up everything to do this, but we will have to give up that which causes us to sin. It's that tendency to sin that can effectively derail all of our good efforts. A little bit of sin can go a very long way toward ruining our efforts in working with and for God. It's those sinful tendencies that other people can see so easily in us that can destroy our future with Him.

As unfair as it may seem, we Catholics are under a microscope when it comes to our behavior. If we're going to be His ambassadors, we cannot allow ourselves to consciously indulge in habits that offend God. While we cannot be perfectly sinless, we must always be conscious of our sins and be quick to correct our mistakes. In this way, we can develop a close walking faith with God.

This process is not an established program; one size does not fit all. The first thing a person must do however is probably the hardest. He or she must turn from the things they are currently doing that upset God and look for re-establishing or building up their current relationship with Him. It is as I said earlier; we are like the prodigal son or daughter. We have to return home and ask for forgiveness. Once we do this, God will then take us under His wing and teach us as He did with the Disciples.

What prevents us from doing this is what we need to talk about next. All of our Christian beliefs are worthless unless we can use and apply them where we live and work. Since there are distinct barriers that will block us, it makes sense that we should study and understand them, in preparation of the times you will encounter them (and you will). I can truthfully say that I have personally experienced each of the ones that follow as well as through my clients and friends. I hope that these situations are familiar to you and that you can relate to them. I also hope my comments help you in your own developing walk with the Lord.

Barrier 1: What Have We Done to God?

My formal education in the Catholic faith ended in the late 1960's, right about the time Vatican II's changes began to take root. My generation's way of thinking, distinctively grounded in the Catholic faith, was soon to be a thing of the past. The old style catechism, core principles of the Faith, belief in the absolute authority of the parish priest, familiar customs, traditions and teachings were all being loosened from their age-old moorings. They were seen more as optional or suggested behavior rather than mandatory.

Since then, many who grew up with a Catholic education have received something other than a solid grounding in the core principles of the Catholic faith their parents knew. While I applaud the efforts of the Catholic Church during Vatican II, there were some unexpected results. When we attempted to modernize the old core teachings and customs of the Church after Vatican II, simply put we ended up demoting God. We actually took away some of His power and majesty. For those who were learning about Him for the first time, God and His Son were in the process of becoming more and more irrelevant to the core principles of the Catholic faith. Since many people object to God being the ultimate judge and Jesus being the only way into heaven, these two facts alone have been de-emphasized from the church pulpits of America.

I remember teaching CCD to eighth graders in the early nineties and being struck by how un-mighty, un-sacred, un-special and un-useful God had become in their eyes. In essence, He became a kind of "superman" whose powers were minimal and useful only on occasion. For many, God truly became irrelevant. Many teaching materials portrayed Jesus more as a "good guy" rather than a good God. Gone was the emphasis on God, the omnipotent, all-knowing, all-loving, all-seeing, Creator and Savior of the world.

Instead, the emphasis has been on social justice and the care of others. These ideas in and of themselves are hardly wrong. But these things are to be accomplished as a result of our close relationship with God and respect for Him, not in place of that relationship. They are the "fruit" or consequence of a close walking faith with God.

The key in any relationship with God is the recognition that He is our God and we must live according to His laws and ultimately answer to Him. The first instruction in the book of Proverbs states,

The fear of the LORD is the beginning of knowledge; fools despise wisdom and instruction.

PROVERBS 1:7

Fear of the Lord is simply respect and admiration for God, His position as creator, His sovereignty and His goodness toward men. This becomes the basis upon which we can interact and worship God. Starting off on any other footing condemns our relationship to failure. Once we eliminate reverence, respect, awe and wonder of God's majesty, we've taken God down to the level of man.

Many Catholics in post-Vatican II generations have the wrong notions and beliefs about our Lord and Savior. They cannot see any rational, practical reason for putting Christ or God first in their daily lives. Why would they if they believe that God is not all that almighty or powerful or concerned about us here on earth? If they've been taught that it's mainly up to them to solve their own problems, why should they give God prominence in their personal lives?

There now seems to be two competing approaches to Catholicism: one stressing care of the needy and the other promoting a form of self-reliance. Both approaches shift our focus from dependence and reliance on a supreme creator to ourselves. I believe this effort has resulted in the sometimes justifiable criticism of Catholics as being mainly works-oriented and not God-dependent.

Many of our era also feel that we are too advanced technologically to believe in some of the old Catholic fundamentals such as the concept of the Trinity, the real presence of Christ in the Eucharist, the necessity of Confession and eternal condemnation to hell if you die with a mortal sin on your soul. Homilies heard in many churches have also been "toned down," de-emphasizing such core beliefs because they may be offensive to some. Is it any wonder, then, that many people today do not see the value or need for a vibrant living faith in God?

In our attempt to make the Church more "user friendly" we have discarded and de-emphasized many of the core fundamentals of our faith commonly taught before Vatican II. So now when a high-ranking church leader—even the Pope himself—publicly states the Church's position on a life issue, Catholics who do not agree simply shrug it off and do as they please. They no longer see God or the Church as having any authority in their lives. We have, in our minds, made God our servant. It's as if He was very useful to us years ago, but today we have much more effective tools and responsive products at our disposal.

But when a catastrophe such as the September 11, 2001 occurs, whom do we call on first? That's right—God. So where does this leave us? It leaves us in a bad position because it is the first and probably biggest barrier to successfully living out our faith. We cannot be living examples of God's word without believing totally in the supremacy of God, Jesus Christ and the Holy Spirit. If the Trinity is weakened in our eyes, our faith becomes rootless, useless, and unable to grow. And what would be the point of having a close walking faith with a diminished God?

In days of old, people were obligated to bow or kneel in the presence of a king or queen as a sign of respect, obedience and allegiance—and to tell the world that they submitted to that royal authority. How often do we as Catholics submit publicly and privately to God in all that we say and do? Is your belief in God strong enough to drive you to live daily according to His will? Don't ignore this question, it's more important than you might think. While you still have a chance, now is the time to consider your answer.

Barrier 2: Work—A Place for Faith?

Bringing your faith to work is rarely easy to do. There is a widespread notion that there is no proper place at work for any kind of religion or expression of faith. Clients, customers and employees who do not approve or agree will be offended. The biggest mistake people of faith make is to assume that they first have to tell others about what they believe. Consider the words of Saint Francis of Assisi:

"Always preach the Gospel; use words when necessary."

I cannot over-emphasize the importance of this advice. I've learned that we have to live the Word before we can speak about it. If we don't, then our words may be received as, "Do as I say, not as I do."

So many Christians fail to grasp the enormous implications of this truth. We would never dream of competing in college or professional level sports unless we were thoroughly prepared and trained. We wouldn't want to embarrass ourselves. But when it comes to matters of faith, for some reason, we feel that we do not need to prepare much at all. But the stakes far, far exceed the outcome of any sporting event. We're dealing with peoples' souls and where they'll spend eternity!

Before you attempt to bring your faith to work, consider devoting some serious prayer time to the endeavor—better still, get a team of people to pray with you and for you. If there are people at work with whom you have already connected on a spiritual level, consider approaching them and enlisting their help in the prayer effort. This can prepare the hearts and minds of the people you'll encounter on the job who need to hear the Gospel message. They'll be more likely to accept what you are telling them. Ask your team to pray that you will be able to respond to the questions and comments of others as Jesus would respond. This is vital—we all need supernatural help to do God's work well.

Always be gentle and listen more than you talk, especially when someone takes you into their confidence about issues important to them. As someone speaks to you, keep one ear on God and the other ear on the person. Believe it or not, this is possible. It's called double tasking and God actually helps us do it when we're working with people in this manner. Remember, you are probably not going to have the absolute correct answer for that person's problems. Sometimes it's not about having the answer, but about listening and being available for that person in need. So get used to the idea of leaning on God for compassion and the proper response.

After reading *In His Steps*, I realized that God wanted me to conduct my work relationships as a true Christian would, not simply as a means to an economic end. Since we are all God's children, every person I encounter is a major concern for God. He wants each one of us to come home to Him in the end.

You don't bring your faith to work, then, just because it sounds like a good idea. You do it because you want to be God's hands and feet. We are His instruments here on earth. This makes even greater sense when you consider that work is where most of us spend the great majority of our waking hours. God's Word and message is true whether it is revealed in a church building or in a work setting. How can anyone who does not attend church come to believe in God if they do not hear His name and His Word out in public? For example, if we don't pray before meals at home or in a restaurant, or before we take a long trip, then how will they learn of Him?

That eighth grader was right. We need to make God more visible so that others will believe He's real and will want to come to know Him on a personal level. Jesus says it plainly:

You are the light of the world. A city built on a hill cannot be hid. No one after lighting a lamp puts it under the bushel basket, but on the lampstand, and it gives light to all in the house. In the same way, let your light shine before others, so that they may see your good works and give glory to your Father in heaven.

MATTHEW 5:14-16

We are without a doubt the light of which Jesus speaks. Ask yourself: How important is light when there is nothing but darkness all around us? What's it like to be in total darkness and not know where to go or who to listen to?

Being the light gives those who take the risk in presenting the Gospel message, a real sense of purpose in our lives. Bringing our faith to work raises the awareness of others to the presence of God. He gives to us, His disciples, the keys to His Kingdom. Among those keys are the people we can minister to.

It's a fallacy to think we need only to live out our faith at home or in private. We need to do it in all situations and all places. But be especially careful when you recreate or socialize, when we typically let our guard down and try to relax. These are the times when we might fall into the trap of going along with the crowd and end up compromising our message too. Hold to your standards and remember who you represent. You are an ambassador of Christ!

Barrier 3: Faith—Too Personal to Share?

Similar to the previous barrier, is the perception that our faith is a very personal and private thing and does not belong out in public. This is only partially true. My relationship with God is personal and private. But how I serve Him can often be a very public thing.

Think about Christ. His relationship with His Father was very private. He spent much time with Him in prayer, private prayer. But then He always returned to the people and lived out His faith, serving His Father publicly. Even His death was the most humiliating kind of public punishment the Romans could administer.

Obviously, we don't do all of our work for God in a public way, but we certainly should not avoid that kind of work because others can see us doing it. Remember what Jesus said in Matthew 5:16 as listed above: The whole point in going public with our faith is to bring glory to God. We let other people see the goodness of God through our actions and reactions. When we act correctly, it gives honor and distinction to God's name and character. It draws people to God. Because of what we do and say, others should want to become Catholics.

It's just like the way we treat our families. Because we love them so much, we do a great deal for family members in an open and public way. Our relationships with one another are personal and private, but others can easily see our personal care and concern.

Remember again that eighth grader in CCD class. Everyone needs to see evidence that God exists. We can be the kind of living proof they need to see about God. Our actions can also tell them that God does love them and that He sends His workers to reflect that love just as a mirror reflects light. It's our love for God that encourages us to be public in our expression of our faith. After all, it's how we often express ourselves to the ones we fall in love with. People who fall in love are easy to spot in public. And so it should be with us when we fall in love with God. Our relationship with Him is very personal, just as it is with the person we fall in love with in life. But in both cases we can express our love out in public.

Remember, He died for us publicly. There isn't anything we shouldn't be willing to do for Him, in private or in public.

Barrier 4: Who Really Is Jesus?

So many people have different and varying perspectives on who or what God represents. But having the correct understanding of God is absolutely critical to our success as Catholics. When you think about it, why should people know anything about God or Jesus Christ? Aside from some churches that actually focus in their services and Bible studies on knowing the Trinity, it just isn't part of our daily informational diet. Even fellow parishioners and other Christians have left me with my jaw on the ground after telling me who they think God is and what they think He is like.

The Bible describes God as a supernatural being having many different aspects or characteristics to His nature. He is unchanging, possessing supreme knowledge of all things past, present and future. He is all-wise, all-loving, gracious, jealous, full of goodness, and He will deliver justice to those who have not repented of their sins.

These are but a few of God's traits. But how often do we hear of people just focusing on one or two traits such as His love and mercy? George Barna of Barna Research conducts polling on Christian attitudes towards matters of faith. In a poll whose results were reported on October 8, 2002 (Americans Draw Theological Beliefs from Diverse Points of View), Mr. Barna reports:

"Although most adults are aligned with either a Protestant (54%) or Catholic (22%) church, a large minority of Americans believes that when Jesus Christ was on earth He committed sins. Currently, slightly less than half of the public (42%) holds this view, while half (50%) say Jesus did not sin." [2]

In another survey released October 21, 2003, (Americans Describe Their Views About Life After Death), he reports:

"Millions of Americans have redefined grace to mean that God is so eager to save people from Hell that He will change His nature and universal principles for their individual benefit. It is astounding how many people develop their faith according to their feelings or cultural assumptions rather than biblical teachings." [2]

These kind of findings go back to my theory of spiritual consumerism. If no one is publicly explaining and living out the truth about God, then we are likely to make up our own truth. We feel we have the license to change things and customize our beliefs to meet our specific needs. I believe this, more than any other Church issue, is for the most part being ignored and its corrupting impact on our society is greatly underestimated by our Church leaders. They do not seem to realize that many people no longer believe in the God of the Bible as presented by Scripture. If you want proof, just visit George Barna's Web site, www.barna.org. The statistics he presents all confirm a slow but definite drift, over the last thirty or so years, away from the fundamentals of Biblical and church teachings, regardless of Christian denomination.

Isn't it interesting? Here we are talking about how to use our faith on a daily basis and one of the most significant barriers stopping us from doing it is we don't know who God is. Go back to your catechism: Why did God make us? To know, love and serve God and to be happy with Him in heaven. If we cannot get past the "know" part, then how can we possibly expect to develop any further in our Christian walk?

But again, why should we know anything about God? Why should our children know anything? Who's talking about God out loud? Between the lack of dialogue on who Jesus is and the fact that relatively few people publicly live out their faith, it's no wonder that people continue to make up their own beliefs about God according to their feelings and desires.

This has to change if we are to store up riches in heaven, as Jesus told us to, and become "rich toward God" (see Luke 12:21). That's who we become if we choose to proceed along the Road to Grace. Since even Christians cannot agree on who or what God is like, we can expect that there will continue to be little dialogue on this topic. Many of us don't want to risk conflict, so we do not talk about the important issues that divide us—or even those on which we agree. Consequently, the general public does not hear any positive discussion about God and matters relating to our eternal disposition. Instead, all they hear are the abundance of bad news stories about the Church. Because of our sinful activities, others may see God as being an accomplice to all the negative activities in Christian churches. He's guilty by association! Consequently, many people no longer care about knowing Him on a personal level.

Many of us can also start to feel that God is irrelevant because

He's nowhere to be found in our daily lives. The things that are truly important to us are always in our daily discussions. If God is not on our lips and in our minds, then He must be extraneous and unimportant to us. This is a prime reason why we as a culture can no longer agree on moral issues that inform our actions. While we haven't yet removed God from His position as the main pillar of Christianity, or even Jesus Christ from His role as Savior, we have changed the functional definitions of both as well as the understanding of their character.

As we discussed earlier, all three persons of the Trinity have been re-described or redefined in our culture. They are now seen by many as being more limited in usefulness, more human-like with the ability to sin or make mistakes and even more likely to ignore certain pleas for help from people. There is also a growing sense of aloofness on the part of God toward our needs.

We Catholics and Christians of all denominations desperately need a common basis for our belief in the Christian God of the Bible. The world needs to see us in agreement on the basics of the Christian faith, even if we still remain split into denominations. Lacking this basic harmony, we not only create all kinds of differences among us but it sends the signal to the world that there is no one true God. Just as we rely on scientists to tell us truthfully how nature works, we look to our religious leaders to guide us truthfully in matters of faith.

As the old saying goes, "When there is a mist in the pulpit, there will be a fog in the pews." If we Christians and Catholics cannot agree on the most common and fundamental parts of our faith, then why should anyone want to become a Christian? As such, we can expect that our Christian faith will become increasingly more irrelevant in the eyes of many as long as we fail to seek common ground on key issues of the Christian faith.

The growth of spiritual anarchy in our society presents a tremendous barrier to learning about God in places where people congregate, such as at work or in social settings. I see Catholics as a particularly hard hit group in this regard. Countless people have left the Catholic Church for other denominations, simply because "they were looking for Jesus." So how can we have a substantive discussion about our faith and who the real Jesus is?

Start by praying that God will bring us together with other brothers and sisters that love the Lord. Look for these people and gather with them. Remember the early Church in Acts 2:42? That's what we need to become right now.

Before you leave for work every day (or for anywhere else), pray ahead of time that you will meet others who believe in Him. Start a Bible study or prayer group in your Church and have one goal: to come to a better knowledge of God. Then build up your faith with whoever comes to those meetings. Work at coming into agreement as to who and what God is. Find and study in detail the Scriptures that reveal His nature. We have to start gathering up the sheep that still believe in the original God, Jesus Christ and Holy Spirit as presented in the Bible. We need to pray with those who are seeking the truth.

And we have to embrace those who admit they no longer know the difference between the God of Abraham and the manufactured god(s) of our present culture. Remember what Jesus said to Peter (and us):

> *Simon son of John, do you love me more than these?*
> *Feed my lambs…Tend my sheep…Feed my sheep.*
>
> JOHN 21:15, 16, 17

If we work at following Christ's commands, His Holy Spirit will always guide us and protect us.

Barrier 5: Differences Among Us

Related to the last barrier is the bigger issue of differences in theological beliefs from one denomination to another. One of the oldest successful military strategies is "divide and conquer." A divided and confused enemy is easier to defeat and Satan has been very effective in dividing God's people.

Personally, I think people will always have a hard time reaching agreement on theological issues. While the great majority of people couldn't care less about Scripture and its interpretation, there are still many who do believe that it not only is the Word of God, but that it also gives us the formulas and advice for successful living. Some of these same people are charged with the promotion of the Gospels and the education of the populace about God.

Too often, some teachers and members of religious orders over-analyze the Scriptures. I find this to be curious because even though Jesus spoke in parables and stories, God meant His laws to be clear and easily understood. After all, whom did He spend most of His time healing and teaching? The poor and discarded people of society—not, generally speaking, well-educated people. Additionally, these teachers of the Law do not realize that their audience is not even paying attention to the most basic concepts. So all of their dissecting and analysis falls largely on deaf ears. As a result, we end up with the phenomenon of having the "saved, saving the saved."

When we dissect the Scriptures word-by-word and interpret every tiny piece of scriptural minutia, we allow ourselves to be distracted from the main purpose of our work: to spread the Gospel and show God's love to one another. Additionally, it drives a wedge between us by giving us much more to disagree over. Or worse yet, we get disgusted with all the squabbling and simply give up. This kind of behavior turns the non-Christian world further away from our faith beliefs.

I am always amazed at how much people know about things that do not matter a whit in the larger scheme of life—sports statistics, for instance, or which celebrities are dating or divorcing—things that will never make any difference in our lives. Unfortunately, this tendency is permeating our spiritual lives as well, as some people dig into the Scriptures and come out knowing as much detail as sports fans who know the batting averages of a baseball player from forty years ago!

Some of these people remind me of the Pharisees of the New Testament—and their behavior can be just as deadly as that of the Chief Priests and Scribes of long ago. If there was a group of people that Jesus really disagreed with, it was the Pharisees and Chief Priests. For proof, just read the twenty-third chapter of Matthew. Nowhere else in any recorded words of Christ was Jesus so profoundly critical of anyone.

I never gave Matthew 23 much serious thought until the day I saw it acted out in a video portraying Christ's life. It was incredible! I was shocked at the names Jesus calls the Pharisees: blind guides, hypocrites, sons of hell, blind fools, snakes, a brood of vipers—to name a few. He also compares them to whitewashed tombs, which look clean on the outside but are filled with the bones of dead people on the inside. To the Jews of His day, this reference was particularly condemning. It showed how far these teachers had gone down the wrong road. They were literally a defilement to the Jewish faith.

But what would make Jesus so upset that He would say such things? We would do well to understand why—here's a list of their tendencies and faults:

- They created their own religious rules and laws in addition to those in Scripture, further burdening the people. Worse, they gave their own manufactured rules equal weight and importance with God's laws.
- Their piety was often hypocritical: They sought to force others to live up to standards that even they couldn't meet.
- They believed that salvation came from compliance with the

laws rather than grace and forgiveness of sins. Furthermore, they were more concerned with the laws themselves than about living out the essence of God's laws and caring for the people. They had little real compassion for anyone.

- They were more concerned about appearing to be holy and good rather than actually being obedient to God. In the process they lost sight of God's message of mercy and grace. They placed themselves before God in importance, rather than teaching others that God is the source of all truth deserving one hundred percent of their attention.

Are we not guilty of the same thinking and behaviors? They're easy traps to fall into and they drive those wedges between us deeper still because they are not based on faith and love. And sadly, they abound in today's world of religion.

Be careful of another trap. If we are working for God, we may figure that there can't be anything wrong with our behavior. Yet nothing could be further from the truth. We must continuously assess our own thoughts and what we are doing, as Jesus commanded His Disciples to do:

> *Go and learn what this means, "I desire mercy, not sacrifice."*
>
> MATTHEW 9:13

He wants us to focus our energies on helping and showing compassion to others.

God's message here is clear. He wants us to be humble and "poor in spirit" so we will not be prideful or personally independent. We instead, must yield to God's will for us. It was the prophet Isaiah who revealed this important fact about God, saying,

> *Turn to me and be saved, all the ends of the earth! For I am God, and there is no other.*
>
> ISAIAH 45:22

If we concentrate our attention daily on God, then we will be saved, plain and simple. When we take our focus off of God we will fall. It was the same for Peter when he tried to walk to Jesus on the water. While he kept his focus on Jesus, he could do it. But as soon as he looked down and around him at the waves, he became frightened and fell.

When we depend on God for our well being, He blesses us. Becoming rich Catholics means that we will store up for ourselves riches in heaven because we are doing what God wants us to do along the Road to Grace. But again, it's a matter of attitude. Being poor in spirit means we relinquish our rights to ourselves. We become poor in our own spirit and we now yield to God's spirit which He places in us. If we allow this to happen, He will bless us with much. But He's also desperately looking for workers, people who are ready to go out and do His work, to feed His sheep and help the lost find their way home:

Then he said to his disciples, "The harvest is plentiful, but the laborers are few; therefore ask the Lord of the harvest to send out laborers into his harvest."

MATTHEW 9:37-38

There comes a time when we have to stop analyzing God's words and just go out and do them. Read the following two key verses:

But be doers of the word, and not merely hearers who deceive themselves.

JAMES 1:22

For just as the body without the spirit is dead, so faith without works is also dead.

JAMES 2:26

Again, God's command here is clear. He wants us to go and put His Word into action. It's not hard to understand, but for many Catholics, it's a very hard thing to do—until we focus on what we all have in common spiritually, with other Christians.

I am convinced that if God returned to earth today, His greatest complaint would be how we, His children and followers have refused to come together on even the basics of our Christian beliefs. Many of us Christians all believe in Him, in the Trinity, in Christ crucified, in the afterlife and many other concepts. So why do we stay apart? Why can't we present a united front of Christian belief to the world just on the issues on which we do agree? Has there ever been a time in all of human history when we needed this more?

It's amazing how much spiritual common ground we share. We just don't know about it because we never talk about it. Talking about it can be time-consuming, inconvenient and even, when we disagree, painful. But the biggest problem is that discussion will threaten the power base of those in charge—another age-old truth about human nature. But remember: As long as we fail to come together for any reason, Satan rejoices and Jesus weeps.

In John 17, Jesus speaks audibly to His Father, praying for unity. Unless we Christians and Catholics come together, the Church of Jesus Christ will continue to separate and come apart. And the disconnection is occurring from within our churches at the very grass roots of many Christian denominations. The Catholic Church does not have a monopoly on this core disease. Many people are disconnecting from their faith, quietly and, in many cases, permanently because they can no longer see the need for faith or can no longer cope with the hypocrisy.

Consider this: If "divide and conquer" is the best military strategy to overcome your opponent, then shouldn't, "in unity there is strength" be our best defense?

Barrier 6: Following Christ, a Risky Business?

This barrier, all by itself, can run a lot of would-be disciples right off the Road to Grace. It almost happened to me.

I became involved with an organization called Fellowship of Companies for Christ International (FCCI)[5], a nondenominational, Christian-based organization whose membership is comprised of Christian CEOs and business owners. Its goal is to promote the Gospel of Jesus Christ by helping its membership learn how to integrate their faith with their work.

At my first FCCI meeting, I became aware that I had undertaken a significant challenge to my newfound faith. There were a number of business owners at that meeting, all with the same notion as me: that God was calling us to bring our faith to bear in our work and business lives. I had never attended any meeting like this. We were gathering to hear what God wanted to tell us as business leaders, as we studied Scriptures and listened to one another's experiences.

During my long ride home that day, I pondered what I had heard. On the one hand, it was exciting being part of a group that was on the cutting edge of a new concept. But something bothered me. All throughout my spiritual life, I always kept a low profile in church, seeking the back of the church and anonymity. I did not want to stand out. Now I was rushing headlong into something that would make my spiritual beliefs a very public thing.

For a Catholic like me, this just felt, well, crazy! I always thought and felt that Evangelicals and maybe even Charismatic Catholics could do the things discussed at the meeting, but not a "mainline Catholic." Catholics like me were just supposed to be there in church on Sundays and holy days. That was our job and our duty. At the meeting we discussed the following verses:

He called the crowd with his disciples, and said to them, "If any want to become my followers, let them deny themselves and take up their cross and follow me. For those who want to save their life will lose it, and those who lose their life for my sake, and for the sake of the gospel, will save it."

Mark 8:34-35

Here was another major barrier in my new walk with God. I came to realize that working for God can be a hard and dangerous business. Why would anyone put all they had on the line for some invisible God and a set of risky theories? After all, just about all of the Saints and real followers of Christ did not live comfortable lives extending into a ripe old age. On the contrary, many of them ended up as martyrs. But Christ knew what people would need to be successful in following Him.

Suddenly, I realized what I had to do. I had to dedicate everything I owned, all my possessions, my business interests, my family, all of my life interests and whatever else I came across in the future, to Him. They were all His anyway; He had merely lent them to me to use as best I could. I decided therefore, to work as hard as I could with what I had, to promote His kingdom. His going to the cross saved me personally, an enormous point many Catholics fail to grasp. He didn't die for us as a group, He died for each one of us.

Could I do anything less in return, if this is what He asked of me? When somebody saves your life, can you deny any request they make of you? Jesus gave me eternal life—wasn't that alone worth the risk of serving Him? Saint Paul puts it this way:

Not that I have already obtained this or have already reached the goal; but I press on to make it my own, because Christ Jesus has made me his own. Beloved, I do not consider that I have made it my own; but this one thing I do: forgetting what lies behind and straining forward to what lies ahead, I press on toward the goal for the prize of the heavenly call of God in Christ Jesus.

PHILIPPIANS 3:12-14

Now see how clearly this is stated in *The Message:*

I am not saying that I have this all together, that I have it made. But I am well on my way, reaching out for Christ, who has so wondrously reached out for me. Friends, don't get me wrong: By no means do I count myself an expert in all of this, but I've got my eye on the goal, where God is beckoning us onward—to Jesus. I'm off and running, and I'm not turning back.

PHILIPPIANS 3:12-14, *The Message*

We are all called to pick up our crosses and accept them for Christ's sake—to be sure, a very frightening prospect for most of us. But consider this: Who in life has had it easy? Who do you know who has not had any difficulties or crosses to bear? I know of no one. Furthermore, I have yet to meet the person with whom I would like to trade places. I know of no one who is "set for life," even with all the money in the world.

So it is well that we, like Saint Paul himself, dedicate ourselves to God's work even if it means experiencing some difficult times. We'll always have tough times to endure. Knowing that we are going through a trial that will benefit God's plan for the salvation of all can become a joyous sacrifice.

Jesus told us that if we protect and cherish the things we've gained and achieved in this life more than our love for Him and the Gospel, then we will probably lose our eternal life. Why? By protecting our personal assets, however hard we worked to earn them, we will have placed more value on the things of this world than on the things of God's world. We will not have trusted and yielded ourselves fully to God. Conversely, if we commit everything we've gained to God, then He will assure us of eternal life. It's simply a matter of choice.

Depending on which choice we make, our lives eventually follow a theme determined by the things we value the most. And God sees whether we treasure the same things He treasures. The catechism of the Catholic Church makes an interesting point regarding Mark 8:34 as it relates to marriage vows. But it also pertains to anyone embarking on the Road to Grace:

> It is by following Christ, renouncing themselves, and taking up their crosses that spouses will be able to "receive" the original meaning of marriage and live it with the help of Christ.
>
> (CCC 1615)

Notice the last few words. If we commit to Christ in marriage and on the Road to Grace, He will help us. He will provide us with the special graces we need to get through the challenges we encounter and the risk that we take in walking with Him. Realizing this convinced and encouraged me to make my life mean something to God and those around me.

Knowing this now, what will you do?

Barrier 7: Following Christ—a Costly Business?

When we decide to publicly take a position grounded in our faith, it could cost us financially—reason enough for people to think two or three times before sharing their faith with others. We might lose our friends, jobs and customers. If you own a business, you might even get sued by an irate employee or customer who feels that their right to have a religion-free work environment has been violated.

My experience as a business owner has taught me that having the support of all your business partners is vital. Being of like mind and spirit with those who are invested in the business is critical. If you are a sole proprietor (such as an independent contractor), I would suggest that you seek the support of a spouse, a significant other or a "council of advisors," so you can bring your experiences and business plans to other people of like mind and beliefs who understand what you are trying to accomplish.

A council of advisors is a concept I came across while in FCCI. It's a small group (3 or 4 people) of business-minded Christian friends that would act similarly to a board of directors to help guide you in running your business in a godly manner. You actually answer to them in how you run your business from day to day. For business owners it is absolutely critical that they find a small group of like-minded people who are in the same position as they are in their own businesses.

One of the key questions we ask in FCCI meetings is, "What would Jesus do?" This helps us see every business situation we encounter more clearly and from God's perspective. An important benefit of having a group like this is that it promotes accountability for the decisions we make. In fact, this could be a separate barrier all its own.

Accountability is a major stumbling block for people who are in charge of their own businesses. Often we are left to our own judgment about how to handle a business or personnel matter at work. It's generally in the nature of CEOs and business owners to resist being accountable. After all, we rose to our positions because we're independent by nature. But being accountable to someone else helps us make better decisions. It also reminds us that God is the owner of all that we have. We are the stewards and caretakers of the resources He gives us charge over,

For every wild animal of the forest is mine, the cattle on a thousand hills.

PSALMS 50:10

I do not believe a person can be a good Catholic, or Christian for that matter, without being accountable to someone else for their spiritual and physical behavior. Having like-principled peers to advise me on the business issues I face helps me make better business decisions that are in line with God's laws.

Even if you are not a business owner, as an employee you will still have to approach this concept in a similar manner. You will need to lean not only on God for your support but also on others whom you trust. But the best way of overcoming this particular barrier is to work on it with others. With their help and prayers, prepare yourself mentally, physically and spiritually before you try to bring your faith into the public arena. Many of the people who have found that expressing their faith at work too costly, moved too fast and did not prepare themselves well enough for what was ahead of them.

Bear in mind that Jesus prepared His disciples for several years, walking with them, watching their progress very closely and explaining everything. Read the following verses and see what happens when you work and walk closely with God:

> *With many such parables he spoke the word to them, as they were able to hear it; he did not speak to them except in parables, but he explained everything in private to his disciples.*
>
> MARK 4:33-34

We should take great comfort in knowing that in everything we do for Him, His Holy Spirit accompanies us and protects us as God continues to explain things to us in detail. The more we step out for Him at the appropriate times, the more He'll support us. Don't expect Him to give you the whole picture of what He's planning for you. He rarely works that way. He reveals His plan piece by piece and day by day. The more we trust Him, the more He reveals to us. If you need encouragement then just read Jesus' words:

Everyone therefore who acknowledges me before others, I also will acknowledge before my Father in heaven; but whoever denies me before others, I also will deny before my Father in heaven.

MATTHEW 10:32-33

Following God is not an easy task. It will cost us something, somewhere, at some time. Whether you own your own business or work for someone else, the call to spread the Gospel message at work and in other environments is always present for all Catholics. It will cost us; you can count on it. And the cost most always comes because we're called to live the Gospel message every day. If we live it out, others will see that and react to it either negatively or positively. So prepare and plan for it. It is always better to work on overcoming this barrier with the help of others who will support and encourage you.

The Great Commission found in Matthew 28:19 is the common call to all Christians to spread God's Word. How we express that call depends on where we are in our jobs, community and family life. We are all working for Him. So let us support and love one another in this great effort.

Barrier 8: Incorrect Assumptions

Overcoming the tendency of making bad assumptions is a most difficult thing to do. I decided that the best way to discuss it was to relate the experiences I encountered when I tried to "Christianize" our accounting practice. I hope you will be able to learn from the errors I made in my attempt to bring the Gospel message to others in my life. Whether you are trying to bring your faith to work, or want to share the Gospel with friends or even more difficult, want to tell family members about Jesus, the following examples should help you anticipate what you might encounter. As you will see, it is difficult to prepare for every contingency. You just never know how people will react to a spiritual message or conversation about faith. Here again is another reason for maintaining a close relationship with God's Holy Spirit.

My first assumption before introducing my faith at work was that people who go to church regularly like me should recognize the validity of what I was trying to do. I expected that they would welcome the change in our attitudes and mission at our firm. After all, I was introducing a message of hope and fairness in how we treat everyone we meet at work. I also made some other basic assumptions:

- That our employees would understand the Christian message and goals and would eagerly join in or at least quietly support them.
- That our clients, for the most part, would at least welcome a strong ethical business posture even if they did not fully understand or appreciate the spiritual dimension.
- That while obviously not all of our clients and employees were Christian, they would certainly appreciate our desire and right to conduct business in the best of the Christian tradition. After all, it would assure them of more employee benefits and a higher level of quality in our work and professionalism. In short, they would be getting more for their money.
- That I could personally make the mental and psychological change from being the principal owner in charge to the status of being a steward or caretaker of the firm, since now God owned the business. This is one of the key concepts in a successful walk with God—the recognition that everything one has is really His. So it represented a real shift in focus for me.
- That I would and could be accountable to the staff and clients for my actions at work as far as their welfare and the promised level of service were concerned. At the time this assumption did not seem too onerous to me since we were

always trying to do our best for all concerned anyhow.

• That my staff, my partner and I could adapt to these changes with a just little bit of effort.

These, however turned out to be very big assumptions. As a group, our employees didn't know what to make of my newfound faith. They were accustomed to my hard driving, demanding nature. Because I did little to prepare the ground, I think my proposal of bringing my faith to work seemed at best hypocritical to them. It was as if each person sat back and in his or her own mind said "Okay, this ought to be good. You show us the way. We'll watch." I didn't realize what I had done. I had just raised the height of the jumps I had to clear every day in how I dealt with clients and other business matters, but I wasn't in shape to clear them. I felt like I had signed up for Olympic ice-skating after learning to skate only two months earlier!

So everyone was now watching me to see how I'd react to the every day challenges of the business. Would I respond as a new Christian or as the "old boss?" This reminds me of Jesus' wineskin verses:

Neither is new wine put into old wineskins; otherwise, the skins burst, and the wine is spilled, and the skins are destroyed; but new wine is put into fresh wineskins, and so both are preserved.

MATTHEW 9:17

How true this statement is, as I found out much to my discomfort. If we plan to take the new wine of God's words into our lives, we must make sure we have prepared ourselves on the "outside." We must first do away with our obvious sinful habits that others can see and hear, so they can see the changes our faith has made in us. Otherwise we will be attempting to put God's Word into our "old wineskins" and we will break.

One employee, a fairly active Christian, was privately intrigued by my proposal. It was his opinion that this whole effort was a nice thought but that it would never work in a New England accounting practice.

Discussions with our clients were very revealing as well. Some were concerned with what our new spiritual posture meant for IRS audits. Did this mean that we weren't going to be aggressive in defending positions taken on a tax return? Were we just going to acquiesce to whatever the IRS wanted? One fellow actually said, "Wow, does this mean I have to start being honest on my taxes each year?" Another shrugged his shoulders and simply said, "Well, I guess it at least makes you guys look honest."

Overall, most of our clients seemed to ignore our new efforts. We continued to do business as usual, trying as often as possible to apply Biblical principles to our problem solving. But I think more people than we realized were watching us to see if this new approach would work. Like that eighth grader in CCD, they might have been privately hoping we would succeed with this program and prove that God really does exist. This is a very good point for those who want to apply their beliefs. Some people will cheer you on; others will be skeptical at best. I also guarantee you that you will be surprised at who supports you and who doesn't. Because we rarely ever talk about our faith, we don't know who the true followers are and who the make-believers are. However, if you stay on the Road to Grace, you will find out eventually.

Another incorrect assumption that contributed to the failure to integrate our faith and our work was that my business partner and I just assumed that this whole process would work itself out and somehow we would become better business owners and Christians. We thought that since we were at least trying to use our faith in our work, God would bless us and take care of the rest. It was a big assumption and a big mistake.

First, our faiths were at different levels of spiritual

development. Second, our understandings of our goals were also different. Third, we were too busy to focus on this together. We never set enough time aside to just talk and pray together. This is a sure fire way to fail.

But there was another reason why our efforts at living out our faith fell short. Both of us did not realize that we had chosen to step out onto that Road to Grace. I don't think we understood just how serious a challenge it is to truly live out our faith in public—yet this is a critical part of accepting a close, personal walking faith with God.

We needed to go into this kind of a relationship with our eyes open and our hearts ready to give all we had to God. We also had to be ready to yield to His will. In short, we were both very unprepared to undertake this task. If you want to bring your faith into your business, then you need to have your key people on board one hundred percent. They not only have to understand your heart (and you theirs) but they also have to be on the same side of the plan as you. They need to be fairly well grounded in the Scriptures and in their faith beliefs.

If you want to share your faith in a work setting, I would advise you again to prepare the ground with your actions and prayers. How you act toward others goes a long way to showing people what you believe in. A good friend of mine quietly keeps a journal of the various issues and problems she hears about in all the lives of her co-workers. As she gets ready for work every morning, she privately prays over them and asks God to let her know what to say to people in order to help them. When she asks those people detailed questions about how their situations are progressing, she's showing her love and concern and it usually touches them greatly. That in itself is a tremendous witness of her faith. Remember, people don't care how much you know until you first show how much you care.

As I counsel people, I try to remember to pray for them while they are explaining their problems to me. Sometimes, if I feel it is appropriate, I'll actually stop the conversation and ask if they want to pray aloud about their issues with me. These moments can be a very powerful. Read what Saint Peter had to say about taking your faith public:

Always be ready to make your defense to anyone who demands from you an accounting for the hope that is in you; yet do it with gentleness and reverence. Keep your conscience clear, so that, when you are maligned, those who abuse you for your good conduct in Christ may be put to shame.

1 PETER 3:15-16

We must always be prepared to share what we believe and why—not to defend our spiritual actions but more because we are called to teach people about God. There is a tremendous hunger and ignorance in our culture about God. Saint Peter tells us that we have to be ready to help others learn about God and the Gospel. And we need to do it in a way that invites them to ask more questions.

If you decide to pray with people, then you'd better be ready to explain yourself and what you are doing. For example, whom are you praying to? Was it Jesus, Buddha, the God of the Bible or someone or something else? There may even be others within earshot of your conversation and suddenly you're on stage and you have maybe only ten, twenty or thirty seconds to get the words out in such a way that they'll understand or at least be intrigued by what you are saying. If this happens to you, first pray quickly for God to give you the words before you say or do anything, then listen to what the Holy Spirit tells you as you begin to speak.

Another tip is to practice for this moment. Get the basics of what you would say on paper and memorize the important points that you want to stress. You may even want to draw a simple picture to illustrate a point. Pictures can remain a long time in peoples' memories. This is a tough barrier; don't underestimate it.

Remember, people today are like the prodigal son. In many cases, they have been all over the world and in and out of all kinds of relationships. Their experiences will usually differ greatly from yours so their assumptions about spiritual matters will also differ from yours. Always try and find out where they are in their thinking and concerns before you talk to them about faith matters. Very importantly, this gives you the chance to prepare the ground by praying for them and their specific issues. It also gives you time to hear God tell you what to say to them and how to help them.

Finally, try not to assume anything about anyone anymore. Instead, work on opening your heart and mind to God and prepare to receive and pass along what He has for each person you stop to help. It worked for the Good Samaritan and it will work for you.

Barrier 9: Ethics and Walking With God

In the wake of Enron, WorldCom, Tyco, Putnam and all of the other recent business scandals, a key question from a strict business perspective is whether or not we really need to bring our faith into the places where we work and socialize. Since it can cause so much controversy, how can it possibly be of real economic value to the company and the people employed there? After all, if we just stay close to God in our own hearts and thinking, isn't that enough? Can't we just be personally responsible for our own lives, jobs and families?

At a statewide bankers' symposium I recently attended, our State's Bank Commissioner started his keynote talk with a question:

"Ladies and gentlemen, I just want to know one thing. What the hell is going on out there? In the last 6 years over 54% of all bank failures in our country have been caused by fraud. And the people doing these things are the big boys, the people who handle billions of dollars each day. What the hell is going on?"

I wanted to leap out of my seat with the answer. Just the night before, I had begun teaching an accounting course at a local state university. I asked the students, all of whom were approximately twenty years old, to define ethics. No one could answer. A few had heard the word somewhere before but none could discuss what it meant. I ask this question every semester, by the way, and usually get a similar result.

The answer to the Bank Commissioner's question is this: the disease of not knowing God has progressed so far, that it now manifests itself in the form of our not even knowing what is right and wrong. And this condition has now made its way into the business world to the point where it is easily seen in more and more business situations. Ethics is not being taught in the classroom to any significant degree because we've given up on teaching about God. The two issues are tied together. Ethics springs from a knowledge base of moral principles that point toward the differences between right and wrong. And spiritual matters are what shape our moral principles.

Many of us don't realize that "good" comes from God. He is the source of all that is good, right and correct. If we eliminate God from the public portion of our lives, then we'll never learn and will be unable to teach others what is right behavior and what is wrong. Our supreme spiritual authority for these truths will be gone. We'll be left only with a human level of authority.

God owns the spiritual world. Anything of value we hope to gain from that world needs to come from Him. But very few people are putting this together. The very basis for our moral behavior is spiritual! Where do the building blocks of our moral belief system come from? Whose laws are we going to obey? Whose values are we going to promote?

If ethical principles are not based on a solid belief in a higher Creator, then what force of authority can stand behind them? If it isn't God, then it has to be the IRS, the FBI, the State Police and other man-made agencies. The fear of getting caught is today the only basis for moral and ethical behavior. Our first and strongest line of defense, fear (reverence) of God and His laws seems all but gone. What's left is the fear of getting caught. And because the odds are good that people won't get caught, they are willing to take a chance and commit fraud. Just about every semester my students tell me honestly, "Do whatever it takes, but don't get caught." I see this kind of thinking and behavior in too many of my clients as well.

But do you know what else I pick up from my students? I hear their answers, but they often end with question marks. They're not sure about their answers because something deep inside them, perhaps the remnants or beginnings of a conscience, tells them that their answers might not be right. Here's the eighth grader from CCD class again. They want to be shown the truth. We who run the world's institutions have to prove that the truth exists by living it ourselves!

Consequently, we, the investors, are in trouble on Wall Street. The people who are in charge of caring for our investments don't know how to stop the fraud and the scandal. But I do know another way that will work. We have to get back to our spiritual roots. What would Jesus do? Well, He certainly wouldn't cheat, steal, lie, testify falsely, exaggerate the truth, slander and malign others, step on His friends to get ahead, or be totally consumed with gaining prestige and power.

For quite some time now, I've harbored a radical idea for businesses. I suggest that they offer their staff religion classes.

That's right: Give them a sense of their duty to the God of the universe and to their fellow man. The classes can be held at area churches where the company's employees attend regular services. The company could fund the classes and attendance would be strongly encouraged by management. Investors will love it because they will see it as a way to prevent theft and fraud. How much could it cost? Nickels and dimes compared to the cost of just one major theft. Besides, every major world religion speaks against stealing and fraud. I know this is radical but don't we need to try something?

Our faith is critical in our work. We are spiritual creatures; this needs to be recognized and exercised. Call it ethics; knowing right from wrong, doing the right thing, walking with the Lord, following Christ, developing a close personal relationship with Jesus—it makes no difference. God is the source of all that is good. No one can ever change that fact. Remember chapter 15 in the Gospel of Saint John? Jesus tells us in black and white,

I am the vine, you are the branches. Those who abide in me and I in them bear much fruit, because apart from me you can do nothing.

John 15:5

These words are either true or false. If they're true, then they'll apply to Wall Street, the place where we work as well as to all the other parts of our lives.

Barrier 10: Excuses, Excuses

Excuses are easy for us all to make. Our lives are hectic and it's easy to say we're too tired or too busy—and truthfully, many of us often are. But beneath the surface of these excuses lies a real problem. We have become too absorbed with our worldly habits and ways of thinking. It's natural for us to want to "feather our nests." But material pursuits can have very little to do with God's plans and agenda for us. A friend once told me, "Whenever I find myself in a situation where everything is going my way and in a sense, I am in step with the world, then I know that I'm probably in big trouble with Jesus."

We know what God is expecting from us. We just don't realize how present He is in our daily activities. He is with us and He does see our every action and thought. We get so involved in certain things that we don't even wonder where God is in our lives. We don't miss Him until something goes wrong.

Remember the old adage, "Idle hands are the devil's workshop?" I believe that today the adage should be, "Busy hands are the devil's workshop." Why? Because Satan knows this is the best way to separate us from God. By keeping very busy with things in our daily lives, even good things, we have little time or energy left for the best things God wants in our lives.

Satan's job is to populate hell. Our unprecedented levels of wealth, recreational toys, second homes, exotic vacations and the like take time to care for and to enjoy. They consume large amounts of our thought, time and resources, leaving us little or nothing to give the needy person right in our own businesses, communities and families—the very people God wants us to care for. As a result, we keep ourselves too busy for any intimate contact with God.

For example, this distractedness is particularly evident in the area of healing prayer, as I've seen in my involvement with "The Oratory of the Little Way," a small, residential Christian healing center in Connecticut. Many have come to the Oratory with terminal diseases and received a healing through prayer. But some do not understand who or what healed them. We explain that it is by the power of the Holy Spirit that healing can happen. But they find that explanation confusing or difficult to understand. So many of us have avoided meaningful and personal contact with God for so long, that we can no longer recognize

Him when He personally intervenes in our lives. We may not even be acquainted with Him enough to say thank you, when we are healed of a life-threatening disease. We've become so busy with so much that we do not and cannot identify what's taking us away from the greatest love of our lives. How sad for us, but how wise a strategy for Satan.

Here's an interesting way to think about this barrier. In order to get closer to Satan and further away from God, we need to make certain that we get over-involved in community affairs, get on more boards of organizations than we should, take up a sport that'll require us to practice and play a great deal without any family involvement. We should also take on more responsibilities at work without creating the compensating balance in time at home. We should be sure we are totally exhausted at the end of every day, so when God does ask us to do something important for Him, we'll be too busy, tired and financially over-extended.

Now, be honest. Does any of this sound familiar? Life is a real tightrope walk these days and the key to success is to always keep our balance. But if we do not start with God, we get out of balance immediately. The more we weigh ourselves down with responsibilities and burdens, the more likely we are to fall. Instead, put Him first and then start to construct a daily routine that He wants you to have. There are lots of good things we can get involved with every day. What we should want are the pursuits that are God's best for us. That's why the Scriptures say,

> *But strive first for the kingdom of God and his righteousness, and all these things will be given to you as well.*
>
> Matthew 6:33

We must connect with God first, in prayer and through those closest to us. When we prayerfully look for answers, He will reveal them to us. Or we can seek answers after we've become over-involved, over-committed, over-extended financially and emotionally. The answers available at this point are remedies such as divorce, bankruptcy, abortion, medication, psychiatrists, tax attorneys, tax court, IRS repossessions, debt counseling and so on. The choice is ours. Preparing is always easier, a lot less expensive and more comforting than repairing.

Barrier 11: Am I My Brother's Keeper?

Few of us like confronting others about their offensive or improper behavior. Many of us hate getting involved in other peoples' lives for any reason. It is even more difficult when we have to tell friends, employees, customers, etc. that their behavior is unacceptable. Bringing a Biblical sense of right and wrong into such a conversation may jeopardize a friendship or business relationship. So we often avoid the potential conflict by saying nothing. But read what the Scriptures say on this topic.

You shall not hate in your heart anyone of your kin; you shall reprove your neighbor, or you will incur guilt yourself.

LEVITICUS 19:17

Or in more contemporary terms:

Don't secretly hate your neighbor. If you have something against him, get it out into the open; otherwise you are an accomplice in his guilt.

LEVITICUS 19:17, *The Message*

Saint Paul makes the point very clear:

In the presence of God and of Christ Jesus, who is to judge the living and the dead, and in view of his appearing and his kingdom, I solemnly urge you: proclaim the message; be persistent whether the time is favorable or unfavorable; convince, rebuke, and encourage, with the utmost patience in teaching. For the time is coming when people will not put up with sound doctrine, but having itching ears, they will accumulate for themselves teachers to suit their own desires, and will turn away from listening to the truth and wander away to myths. As for you, always be sober, endure suffering, do the work of an evangelist, carry out your ministry fully.

2 TIMOTHY 4:1-5

In other words, we're to go to our friends, employees, family members, etc. and help them see where they have gone wrong—otherwise our silence could make us responsible for the consequences of their sins as well.

This is not a welcomed piece of Scripture. It is a tough message to receive, especially in today's culture where it is no longer politically correct to judge or criticize one another. But do Christians "judge" when they point out issues they see in a person's behavior?

A dictionary defines "judge" or "judgment" as "the act of forming an opinion, estimate, notion or conclusion as from the circumstances, as presented to the mind." It seems to me that if we rush to come to a conclusion before hearing all the details and making every effort to bring the matter to their attention for some corrective action, then yes, we would be guilty of judging someone. It's the same thing as jumping to conclusions. Nowadays we seem to have little patience for the details and little time to hear even some of the major facts. Again, because of the hectic pace of our schedules, we cannot give each other the support we truly need at different times.

Yet the verses cited above tell us that we are to care when our neighbor is doing something wrong and that means we are to care enough so that it moves us to take some action. So we will go to a brother or sister to help them without forming a judgment ahead of time about their behavior. We are to make an effort to understand why they acted in such a way, help them see their mistake (if indeed there is one), and help them ask God to restore what has been lost. God does care about the grievousness of our sins, but He cares most about helping us correct our mistakes and returning to Him because when we are lost, we are indeed in danger of eternal death.

When the prodigal son returned home, his father didn't sit him down and judge him first. He didn't even punish him. Instead, he threw him a party! The father heard and knew that the son was truly sorry for his sins and that he would change his ways from that point forward. The son was truly repentant and that was enough for the father.

We must always lovingly help our brothers and sisters see their errors and then do all we can to help them. But, you may ask, many of us have difficulty just dealing with the shortcomings of our own family members. How are we going to affect those outside of our families who we really have no control over?

The answer again comes down to how we live our lives. For example, how often as Catholics do we proclaim the Word as Saint Paul said to Timothy in the above verses? Do we even know what that means? If we don't hear and comply with the simplest of God's commands, then how can we expect to apply the scriptural advice we find in the more difficult verses? Many Bible verses will sound difficult to keep—indeed almost impossible for those who are not attempting to keep God's simpler laws first. The fact is that all of these laws and rules are built upon one another. When we follow God's requests in the simpler laws, He grants us the special graces to abide by the more difficult ones. As we become obedient to God in the smaller things, He then gives us the grace to comply with the more challenging laws. This is what it means to walk on the Road to Grace. More and more "help" from God will come to us as we move closer to Him. If we can do this, then keeping God and His ways in our thoughts and conversation will begin to "rub off" on others. The effect it has is to make them sensitive to God's expectations and love in their lives.

So it follows that if we are working and walking with God, then we will be better able to correct a brother or sister when they get off track. God will give us the resources and ability to do this effectively.

I remember playing a round of golf with a good friend. I just couldn't hit the ball right. I kept putting it in the woods or out of bounds—anywhere but on the fairway. I struggled through almost sixteen holes, until, finally my buddy turned to me and gave me a few tips as to what he thought I was doing wrong. Immediately, I began hitting the ball straight and far. I looked at him with great frustration and anger and said, "You let me go through almost sixteen holes of golf struggling like that and never said anything!"

He sheepishly replied to me, "Well, I didn't want you to get mad at me. I figured you would come around on your own." Does this sound familiar? Don't we "hold back" all too often with those we're supposed to care about? I wonder how much easier life would be if we were more lovingly honest with one another.

To illustrate the point further, let me share a very vivid and disturbing dream I once had. The setting was the last day and God was sitting in His seat of judgment. People were being directed into one of two camps.

To His right went those who had lived their lives in accordance with His laws and spent much of their time and resources in helping those in need. They would accompany God back to heaven at the end of the day. To the left went those who lived their lives mainly in accordance with their own wants and desires and now would be paying the ultimate price for it. They would not be going to heaven.

I felt extremely joyful as I entered the camp on the right and immediately saw a friend I had in life. As we embraced, I looked over his shoulder and to my utter horror, saw people I knew entering the camp on the left. My own intense joy at being saved was tempered by the knowledge that I might have helped save some of those other people from their fate. And I did have opportunities to help them, as some of them had been co-workers, friends, employees and clients. I remember lamenting in my dream, "Oh, why didn't I just try to speak to them when I had the chance?" I don't think I'll ever forget the vividness and message of that dream. Saint James reminds us that we can and should be instruments of the Father. He also indicates that penance for our sins can take a number of different forms.

My brothers and sisters, if anyone among you wanders from the truth and is brought back by another, you should know that whoever brings back a sinner from wandering will save the sinner's soul from death and will cover a multitude of sins.

JAMES 5:19-20

This is good news—we can atone for our sins in a number of ways.

Earlier we noted that the opposite of love is not hate, but indifference. When we say or do nothing to help a brother or sister in need, especially when they need correction, then we are doing just the opposite of what God commanded us to do. This may be the hardest part about your faith walk, but remember that someone's eternal life (not to mention your own) will probably be at stake.

I have yet to meet anyone who has, all by themselves, successfully overcome the barriers we've discussed in this chapter. It takes the grace of God and the support of other believers to overcome these kinds of obstacles. God made us that way. We are capable of achieving anything when we work together just as the twelve Disciples did when they decided to follow Christ. The Great Commission says it plainly, in words aimed directly at us:

And Jesus came and said to them, "All authority in heaven and on earth has been given to me. Go therefore and make disciples of all nations, baptizing them in the name of the Father and of the Son and of the Holy Spirit, and teaching them to obey everything that I have commanded you. And remember, I am with you always, to the end of the age."

MATTHEW 28:18-20

These are Jesus' last words in the Gospel of Matthew—calling us as Catholics to come to His aid or more specifically, to the aid of our brothers and sisters. When we help our brothers and sisters overcome anything that threatens them, we are doing the same good deed to Christ Himself, a fact worth remembering.

The barriers to our faith walk are formidable. But it is time now for us as Catholics to move toward the One who has been personally calling us for so long. Even though we move as one church, He's been asking us to trust Him and follow Him on a personal basis just as he did with the original twelve Disciples. Before He started His ministry, He touched each one of them on a personal level and established an intimate connection. Even on Pentecost, the Holy Spirit came to each person:

Divided tongues, as of fire, appeared among them, and a tongue rested on each of them. All of them were filled with the Holy Spirit...

ACTS 2:3-4

This is what many of us, as "poor Catholics," have failed to see all of our lives. We are not poor. We will not lack anything once we realize who is calling us and once we respond to Him on a personal level. We have the Church, the Trinity, the Sacraments and one another. All we need to do now is realize that we have not been accessing our greatest asset and friend, God through the power of His Holy Spirit. Once we do, we will no longer be poor.

PART IV

FINDING OUR WAY HOME

22

The Bottom Line Question: "Am I Getting into Heaven or Not?"

I am always amazed at the attitude Catholics take whenever we talk about our chances of getting into heaven. I once asked a friend of mine if he wanted to go to heaven when he died, fully expecting that he would say yes. But instead he said, "I guess so." I thought, "What kind of an answer was that?" When I pressed him, he simply said that he had no real feeling one way or another. He felt God was in control of things. He trusted God not to send decent people like himself to a place of eternal damnation and suffering. He was sure that wherever he went in the end wouldn't be so bad. Heaven, purgatory, hell—they were pretty much all the same to him. So why worry about it now?

Others have told me that only very holy people like Mother Theresa go straight to heaven. These are the same folks that feel their best chance for getting into heaven is to aim for purgatory—a risky plan, to say the least. Somehow, they have the impression that purgatory is an easier place to enter because the people that go there were neither very bad nor very good in life. They believe that God would make it an easier place to reach since many more are likely to go there instead of directly to heaven.

A serious problem develops with this kind of reasoning. Once we set our sights lower on a place like purgatory, we feel more at liberty to allow a certain amount of sin into our lives. Subconsciously we reason that since going directly to heaven is out of the question for us and that we're probably going to purgatory anyhow, then we might as well take it easy here in this life. We don't need to go overboard in trying to be too holy.

But suppose purgatory is not that simple a target to hit? How good do we have to be to get into purgatory anyhow? Is it 85% sinless? Higher or lower? Suppose it isn't all that easy to get in there, as is the case with heaven? If we put all our eggs into one basket, so to speak, and we find out that we're not eligible for purgatory, then what? Do we have any options at that point? No, we do not. Our fate is sealed. Our opportunity for making changes is gone. Planning to enter heaven via purgatory is fraught with risks and problems. There has to be a more reliable way.

Then there are some who feel that God would never allow anyone to go to hell. They reason that in the end He will, in some grand, sweeping motion of clemency and grace, throw open the gates of heaven to all regardless of how they lived their lives. And if that doesn't happen, they say, then He surely will accept them on their own personal merits. After all, they didn't spend their lives raping, pillaging and plundering. The vast majority of us aren't that bad! This expectation, though, ignores the entire sacrifice Jesus Christ made for us and contradicts all of what Scripture teaches us. If God knew ahead of time that in the end He would relent and open the gates to heaven to virtually everyone, why would He put His Son through the horror of the Passion and Crucifixion? No, the price God paid was too high.

Then I ran across another fellow who felt his sins were so great that he couldn't even go to Confession. He was afraid of telling another person his darkest secrets. He expected never to gain heaven. He didn't even know that he could have a walking faith with the Lord. He had never even heard of the concept. He was convinced that he would never see God. I explained what it meant to know Christ and suggested he just read the Word and talk with Him in his heart. I also told him that he eventually would need to go to Confession. I hope he heard what God wanted him to hear that day but I remain fearful for him.

I wonder how many other Catholics are out there, with no idea that they can get to know God on a personal basis right here and now. This is how poor we've become as Catholics. We of all people should be the first ones to know how to come to the Father directly. But no one anywhere had ever told this poor man that he could know and walk with God on a personal level. This particular encounter was the final impetus that convinced me to write this book.

How does the question of who is and isn't saved get answered in the end? When I decided to write this book, this question forced me to consider what I really believe about the process of salvation—something I had never fully considered before. Not only did I have to make certain I fully understood it, I had to make sure it made sense and was backed up by Scripture and the Catholic catechism. I also had to feel passionate about it as one does about a personal core belief. I had to honestly ask myself if I was living this belief out in my own life. Most importantly, I had to start praying over this whole process of revealing my belief to you, the reader. I have not stopped praying, even as I type this section.

As I understand it, there are four parts to the process of salvation.

Part 1: For me, the target is heaven. I fully expect to go there at my death. Why? Because I've decided to dedicate my life to God and to do what He wants me to do. I want to live my life in such a way that it pleases God, not so much because I fear the prospect of hell, but because I have developed a genuine love for Him just as I know He has for me. I plan to do all that I can to follow His laws and please Him out of respect for that love. He in return has placed His grace in me and has saved me from eternal death as I move along the Road to Grace. But understand this critical point: He put His grace in me simply because I asked Him to, directly and personally.

Part 2: Once I took that first step of faith and declared God to be my personal Lord and Savior, His unmerited gift of grace began to operate in my life and actually helped me continue to build a faith in Him. This is where those three levels of belief we spoke of earlier come into the picture. As is the case in the first level of belief in God, His ways began to make more and more sense to me. The further along I grew in this relationship with God, the greater my belief grew because I was now developing a closer and a more personal knowledge of God.

Part 3: As my faith grew, I became more passionate about God in my life. As a result, more grace continues to flow toward me and my love for Him grows proportionately. This is the second stage of belief we spoke of earlier. My developing love for God prompts me to look for ways to please Him, just as our love for certain people in our lives moves us to show that our love is real. Because of this love, I now reach a point where my behavior, starts to change for the better.

Part 4: In addition to the good things I've already done in my life, I begin to do more and more good works because I want to please the one I care about the most. This is the third level of belief we discussed. However, it is not my works that save me. It is all God's grace and grace alone that provides me with my salvation. My works become a form of proof or evidence for all (including God) to see. They confirm or deny my statements of belief in God. As a Christian, my actions speak louder than my words, and my actions are critical. Throughout this whole process, I have remained on the Road to Grace and it will eventually lead me home to be with Him forever.

In summary, the grace I initially receive from God builds up my faith base in knowledge of Him. It goes on to build a desire in me to love God in return for His love for me. As I look to express my thanks for this love, I naturally show my love for others by doing good works that help them.

When we find Christ on a personal level, many things occur. One very important revelation is that we finally begin to realize the enormity of what Christ saved us from—the horror of hell—by going to the cross. Many in our culture today choose to de-emphasize the existence and importance of hell as a possible end result to our lives. In any discussion of the question of salvation, it logically follows that salvation is necessary because we need to be saved from something terrible. I think it would be more than foolish to not consider hell as a reality.

In hell, people experience an eternity of pain and suffering comparable to nothing in this life. Though we do suffer evil and pain in this life, we think that in the end our pain will cease and we will live in peace somewhere. That's just one reason why so few people believe in hell's existence. However, the fact is that all people who do not truly believe in God will be sent to hell.

For it is indeed just of God to repay with affliction those who afflict you, and to give relief to the afflicted as well as to us, when the Lord Jesus is revealed from heaven with his mighty angels in flaming fire, inflicting vengeance on those who do not know God and on those who do not obey the gospel of our Lord Jesus. These will suffer the punishment of eternal destruction, separated from the presence of the Lord and from the glory of his might…

2 THESSALONIANS 1:6-9

As we read this Scripture and pray, we start to get an inkling of the dreadfulness of hell—or of what eternity away from God would be like. That's when we begin to realize what Christ did for us. As hell has no parallel to anything we know here on earth, the events of Good Friday have no parallel in all of history. So when a person comes to Christ on a personal basis, he or she actually begins to understand more about who God is and what He has done for each one of us. He saved us from hell.

This is another good reason why we need to know God and come to Christ in a personal way. Jesus personally died for us on the cross. He didn't do it by using other means or persons through proxy or substitution. He did it Himself, of His own personal free will. Once this point finally makes it into the core of our understanding, it then becomes a natural response for us to want to give back all we can to Him. (If someone actually saved your life, what wouldn't you do in return for that person?)

Additionally, we cannot attain any significant progress unless we undertake this whole process of salvation on a personal basis. We must show Him we are willing to personally die to sin as well.

These concepts are important, as they are at the core of our Catholic beliefs. Let me reiterate them in another way: the question is, "What must we actually do to gain salvation?" As Catholics, we believe that we are saved by grace. It is 100% God's mercy and compassion—nothing else—that saves us from eternal damnation. We cannot save ourselves except by reaching out and taking the hand of Christ and allowing Him to save us,

For by grace you have been saved through faith, and this is not your own doing; it is the gift of God—not the result of works, so that no one may boast.

EPHESIANS 2:8-9

But there is one thing that we must do, in order to make this gift of grace operational in our lives. We have to accept it. We choose to accept it by literally saying to God, "Yes, I want your gift of salvation; I believe in you as the God of the Bible and I want to dedicate my life to you."

We must also make a serious Act of Contrition at this time. We must promise God that it is our desire to begin to turn our lives around by moving away from sinful behavior and to start following Him. When we do, we reach that first level of belief we spoke of earlier. Acceptance of God's grace will now make logical sense to us and so we respond to it positively. God then responds to our statements and action with an outpouring of His Grace. This begins the process known as justification which allows us to stand before God.

Justification happens when we agree to become converted and reborn. We go from a life of sin to a new life in which God forgives us. We agree to turn from our sinful ways and we begin to get closer to God in all that we do. Over a lifetime, justification profoundly affects our whole being and—because we now have a faith and belief in God—ultimately prepares us to meet God face-to-face in eternity. But we are not justified because of anything we do even after we stop living a life of sin. We are justified simply because of the ultimate sacrifice Jesus made on our behalf on the cross. Our acceptance of God's grace indicates to Him that we want to change and move toward Him. Our actions then confirm our intentions.

And this then brings us to one other important piece that's needed in this process: our good deeds. We are not saved by our deeds; but they serve as evidence of the reality of our faith and belief in God. They provide visible proof of what we personally claim about God to others around us.

During this process of salvation, our faith continues to grow as we read Scripture and pray to God for our needs and the needs of others. Our attendance at Church and frequent reception of the Sacraments all help us move along and develop a walking faith with God. We literally walk through each day with Him in our thoughts and governing all of our actions. As a result of our belief, good deeds, prayers, Scripture study and regular worship, we start to feel more passionate about our belief in and love for God. We feel the urge to do more and more good works for others. This is the second and third levels of belief—-passionate belief followed by belief put into action.

Our passion for God grows and our desire to serve Him increases. This part of the process is called sanctification—through God's grace, our belief and our behavior, we become more and more like Christ each day. At the end of this process, we have become so much like Christ that we are now fully justified before God and we gain eternal life.

Another important function our works play in the process of salvation is that they bring our desires and will under control. By continually doing things that help others and show God's love in us, we bring the spiritual side of our life into close alignment with our actions—as we get closer to becoming wholly righteous before God.

In summary then, we get into heaven when we connect with God on a personal level—and keep that connection active and alive throughout our entire lives. Remember, though, that this process began simply because God originally put His grace in us after we gave Him our permission to do so. You might want to think of this part of the process as conversion, our turning from sin and stepping onto the Road to Grace that God offers us. Our initial step toward God invites His grace which actually causes our faith to grow and gives us the desire to go about doing good things for people. Justification doesn't end until we are completely sanctified—the state in which we would be just like Christ to those around us.

How important then are our works to our salvation? Consider how important they were for Jesus. He healed and cared for so many people. His whole ministry was noted for His compassion and good works.

Great crowds came to him, bringing with them the lame, the maimed, the blind, the mute, and many others. They put them at his feet, and he cured them, so that the crowd was amazed when they saw the mute speaking, the maimed whole, the lame walking, and the blind seeing. And they praised the God of Israel.

MATTHEW 15:30-31

And Saint James makes it very clear that having a faith without the works is useless,

For just as the body without the spirit is dead, so faith without works is also dead.

JAMES 2:26

Many people throughout history have moved along this path. Mother Theresa is one of the most recent. Clearly, God views good works as a critical result of our encounter with His grace as we move along the Road to Grace. We will produce good fruit and good works if we stay connected with God.

Beware of false prophets, who come to you in sheep's clothing but inwardly are ravenous wolves. You will know them by their fruits. Are grapes gathered from thorns, or figs from thistles? In the same way, every good tree bears good fruit, but the bad tree bears bad fruit. A good tree cannot bear bad fruit, nor can a bad tree bear good fruit. Every tree that does not bear good fruit is cut down and thrown into the fire. Thus you will know them by their fruits.

MATTHEW 7:15-20

The threat to our success in producing good fruit, as God defines it, is our free will. Our free will never gets "trumped" or made inoperative as long as we maintain all of our mental faculties. Consider the two thieves on the crosses next to Christ. Their free wills operated up until the last moment. One used his free will to choose Christ and the other did not.

But I've always wondered about the reverse situation. If faith without the works is dead, what if I have works without the faith? What if I am constantly doing good things for people but have a shallow faith in God? If I don't believe in God to the point that I trust Him implicitly, then can I legitimately say I have a faith? A dictionary will define "faith" as "a confident belief in the truth, value or trustworthiness of a person, idea or thing that does not rest on logical proof or material evidence." Yet many Catholics who are very busy working for God or the cause of God have not committed themselves to Him fully as their Lord, because they have not yet developed a confident belief in the truth of God's existence and laws.

How can that be? It's very simple. Saying we have dedicated our lives to Jesus Christ and that He is our Lord and Savior and actually living as if He is our Lord are two different things. We're probably ready to acknowledge He is our Savior and His death has saved us from the horror of hell. But He is not quite yet our Lord. We are not ready to submit ourselves fully to His will. We want to keep our options open to use our free will whenever we feel it's necessary.

In essence, we have accepted Christ as our Lord and Savior, on our terms, not His. In this case our belief in God has not yet risen to the third level. It is still a shallow belief and it prevents us from fully committing our actions to Him.

Almost one hundred years ago, author and preacher Oswald Chambers in his book *My Utmost for His Highest* described a similar common situation:

> Today we have substituted doctrinal belief for personal belief, and that is why so many people are devoted to causes and so few are devoted to Jesus Christ. People do not really want to be devoted to Jesus, but only to the cause He started. Jesus Christ

is deeply offensive to the educated minds of today, to those who only want Him to be their Friend, and who are unwilling to accept Him in any other way.

Our Lord's primary obedience was to the will of His Father, not to the needs of people—the saving of people was the natural outcome of His obedience to the Father. If I am devoted solely to the cause of humanity, I will soon be exhausted and come to the point where my love will waiver and stumble.

But if I love Jesus Christ personally and passionately, I can serve humanity, even though people may treat me like a "doormat." The secret of a disciple's life is devotion to Jesus Christ, and the characteristic of that life is its seeming insignificance and its meekness. (June 19 reading) [3]

Faith without works is dead. Works without a full abiding faith in God are simply useless. This helps to explain why some people who have been working for God much of their lives, will never see heaven. They have never taken the time to really get to know Him personally and develop a real faith. Reread Mathew 7:21-29. These verses are meant for the make-believers. This is where Jesus talks about people who speak religiously but who do not have a personal living relationship with Him. Consequently their deeds do not reflect the characteristics of good fruit. We must be very careful not to fall into this trap. Working for God does not necessarily mean that you love God. He has said many times,

> *Go and learn what this means, "I desire mercy, not sacrifice."*
>
> MATTHEW 9:13

In order to show compassion for others, we must first be in love with Jesus—there's no other way. My ability to show mercy to others depends on how much I love Jesus and how much of a belief and faith I have in Him.

At what point does salvation actually occur?

That depends on who you ask. Some people believe it occurs at the time you consciously dedicate your life to Christ. They say that once you make that pledge, you are saved and nothing can change that. The Catholic Church on the other hand, believes that salvation is a process that continues throughout your lifetime. Until our final day, the battle will always be between our will and God's will. Just like the two thieves on the crosses next to Christ, their free wills operated up until the last moment. One used his free will to choose Christ and the other did not.

Satan sets a trap with every enticement in order to take us away from our walk with God. Whenever a Catholic chooses God's will over his or her own, a conversion experience takes place. So our salvation is something we have to work at, day in and day out.

This issue, while critical for some Christians, is not a major issue for me personally. Once I made my commitment to Christ, I planned on doing all that I could for Him for as long as I lived. Whether I was saved at the moment of commitment or at some other point in my future does not really concern me. It isn't as if I am going to wave this "deal" in God's face on the Last Day demanding that He let me into heaven because I was saved at some specific time and place. He knows what's best for me, He'll take care of me and that's all I need to know. My concern now is to do all I can for Him. As I said already, we will choose one way or another. With hope, we will see the light in time and accept the gift Christ offers us.

Remember, the prodigal son had to make the initial move to return home. He personally had to choose. We do the exact same thing when we say "yes" to God and ask Him into our lives. We are choosing God over the temptations of this world and this process begins with our saying yes to God and His ways. It continues in a similar manner every day, throughout our entire life.

Yes, there will be times when we wander away from God. We have to be so careful during those times because it is then that the risk of eternal death is greatest. The sooner we return to God in a repentant state, the sooner we become safe and secure again. Saint Paul instructs us to,

...work out your own salvation with fear and trembling; for it is God who is at work in you, enabling you both to will and to work for his good pleasure.

PHILIPPIANS 2:12-13

But I will say it again—Following Christ is not easy. Some people fear that as they continue to develop their faith in God, they will either find the task to be too difficult and return to their old ways, or that they will fail to measure up to God's standards for His disciples. In fact, the Catholic Church teaches that we can lose our salvation even after we accept God's gift of Christ. At any time we can reject that gift through the commission of a mortal sin. Read these two verses carefully:

Note then the kindness and the severity of God: severity toward those who have fallen, but God's kindness toward you, provided you ***continue*** *in his kindness; otherwise you also will be cut off. And even those of Israel, if they do not* ***persist*** *in unbelief, will be grafted in, for God has the power to graft them in again.*

ROMANS 11:22-23, emphasis added

Now I would remind you, brothers and sisters, of the good news that I proclaimed to you, which you in turn received, in which also you stand, through which also you are being saved, if you hold firmly to the message that I proclaimed to you—unless you have come to believe in vain.

1 CORINTHIANS 15:1-2

As I see it, the whole problem stems from our having free will. We have the freedom to choose what we want to do at any time during our lives right up until our death. So at no time does my free will become inoperative unless I decide to truly yield it over to God.

Even if I do, I still have access to that free will and I might reclaim it later on. I can choose to leave my Father, as the prodigal son did. But remember, the son was lost while he was away from his father. He was dead in his sin—the worst possible place to be in one's life. He was headed for hell. Again, we always have a choice to make about God. If we don't want to go to heaven, God will not force us. However, if I do leave Him, I can return to Him. This is the wonderfulness of our Christian faith.

For me, I have decided to ignore this issue. That's right; I just will not allow myself to consider the possibility that I might get caught in this trap. My trust is in the Lord. I trust God to keep me close to Him and take care of me. I have found that when I am in this position, I will never be in danger of being lost. As I said though, some people believe that once they have accepted Christ into their lives, they cannot lose their salvation. I would agree with that statement, as long as they remain close to God in all they do. If you recall our discussion of John 15 and the vine image, Jesus chooses His words very carefully. He tells us to remain in Him or as some older translations have it, abide (to live in) in Him. He says it many times in that chapter. This clearly shows us that He is concerned that we will backslide and leave Him. And He says it plainly,

Whoever does not abide in me is thrown away like a branch and withers; such branches are gathered, thrown into the fire, and burned.

JOHN 15:6

If all it took to gain eternal life was to simply verbally dedicate our lives to Christ, then all of the laws and commandments found in the Bible would be unnecessary. Our response to temptation would as well no longer be a problem and we know that's never true, regardless of how holy we become. Remember, we have control over whether we leave God or stay with Him. He never changes the offer of eternal life to us, but we can change our acceptance of that offer, whenever we see fit. And this is the whole crux of our problem with God, it's our free will.

When you sense any distance growing between you and God, go to Him immediately and restore the relationship. Don't wait! That's the beauty of Catholicism: We have the Sacrament of Reconciliation. We can be restored, as the prodigal son was with his father. This is what we need to rely on in our relationship with God. We should always check to make sure that we are next to Him and walking with Him. If we cannot sense His presence, we must stop what we're doing, find Him and go to Him. Remember, you control the distance between you and God at all times. Just as the father makes it clear to the eldest son that he has always been with Him and therefore was never lost, we need to see our relationship with God in the same way. That's where we want to be, always close to the Father and safe.

In summary then, let's go back to my first grade catechism class. What must I do to save my soul? The answer given is very simple: To save my soul, I must believe in God, I must hope in Him, and I must love Him with all my heart. This is the way we are to live every day.

We would not think of saying the things God wants to hear from us and then go off and live our lives as we want, fully expecting to be safe because we think we're saved! Our love for God needs to be so great that we will do the things He wants every day until we die. Our works and our behavior will always confirm whether our statements to God and about God are true or false. And we will do things for Him not because He saved us at some point in our lives, but because we are in love with Him, plain and simple. As when you fall in love with another person, you always want to be near them and please them. It is the same thing with Jesus, only a great deal more intense. Just remember to always, always stay close to Him.

23

The Road to Grace: The Way to Get Home

Right about now you might be saying to yourself, "I'm ready to do this. I want to step out onto this Road to Grace and make these changes but how do I even begin? I can understand much of what I just read but where do I start and how do I keep it going? If I start trying to make these changes, how does this work with my own Catholic Church? How can I find others who want to do this with me and if I do, is it necessary that they be Catholics?"

These are all good questions, but the primary point here is that you have to decide to make a change. Just like the prodigal son, he reached a point where "he came to his senses…" (Luke 15:17), he decided to make a change. So he got up and started to make his way back home. He too must have had a great many questions on what was to happen.

What I am suggesting here is a very new approach for many Catholics and it's natural that there would be many questions that need to be answered. Consequently, we need to discuss a few things in order to prepare you for what is to come if you decide to pursue a closer walk with God. The process is not an easy one and there will be times when you will be tempted (like Jesus was tempted) to leave and return to your old habits and the old lifestyle you once had. You must not give in to that temptation; it would be disastrous and would cost you greatly.

Probably the biggest obstacle that might prevent your having success is the urge to quit because most of the people around you do not see the need for having a very close relationship with Jesus. For many of us, having a personal closeness with God seems more like an option or choice that only very religious people might want to make. Others may encourage you to take it easy and not be so extreme in your desire to follow Christ. To them, your actions may seem excessive.

In order to see the need to follow Christ more clearly, let's go back to the church model diagram I used earlier.

As I explained, for many years the Church facilitated and intervened as a mediator for us Catholics in the development of our faith with God. We learned from our youth that if we wanted to communicate and interact with God we were strongly encouraged to do so through the Church. We could pray on our own of course, but the Church was where we would go to Mass and partake of the Sacraments as well as worship and pray. The diagram on the right demonstrates a similar situation. As we grow up and become adults, our parents intervene and act as a buffer between us and the world when we are children. They, like the Church, provide for us especially when we are young and immature and this is all well and good.

Now take a look at the suggested new model.

As we all know, there comes a time in the life of most children when they mature to a point when they leave their home and the developmental support provided by their parents. They go off to live their own lives. The relationship with their parents continues, but now it is different. I am sure that most of us would agree that in the great majority of cases, this is a good thing and it is to be encouraged. As seen in the right diagram, the children then have to deal directly with the world around them and "make it on their own."

In a similar way, I am suggesting that we as Catholics have for too long depended mainly on the Church for our relationship with God. It is now time to "graduate" and move out and deal with God directly, one on one. Just as is the case with children and their parents, we must still maintain a loving and supportive relationship with our Church and with God through our church life. We don't leave them; instead, we love them and interact with them even more on a new level.

Interestingly, this analogy goes even further and shows what happens when our parents develop new needs as they age. Obviously we respond to their needs out of love and concern. The same thing should happen with regard to our church relationship; we should provide whatever is needed. Just as we would never think to stay at home and live off of our parents regardless of our age and abilities, we should not treat the Church in a similar manner. If we are capable and not handicapped, we need to connect with Christ directly and develop that relationship. It's imperative for us to develop and mature as Christians so we can become a greater help to the Body of Christ (the Church).

The bottom line is that we need to change our thinking. We must come to our senses and realize that many of us have been "away from home too long." But be very careful here. Many who read this might think they already have an adequate relationship with God and so do not need to go any further. It is my personal belief that very few of us are truly close enough to God. To test this, just ask yourself some simple but probing questions. "Do I read and study the Bible every day? Do I know more about God today than I did yesterday? Am I closer to Him now than ever before? Is He the first one I think of when I wake up every day and the last one I speak to before I go to sleep?"

If you decide that a change is in order for you and you want a closer relationship with God, then start to move forward and let Him provide the answers to your questions. Pray for the answers you need. Pray for the people that would come into your life and work with you as you move along the Road to Grace. Prayer is always the first place to go. As it was when we were children, whenever we had a problem we would go to our parents and ask for help. Similarly, we can also go to our Father and ask in prayer.

A little further on in this chapter, I will give you a practical outline or plan to follow that should help facilitate your walk along the Road to Grace. I call it "The Three Steps Toward Salvation along the Road to Grace." They are a good way to accomplishing what we've been talking about here. But before you start to follow those steps, I would strongly suggest you do something else first.

Take the four Gospels of Matthew, Mark, Luke and John and beginning with John's Gospel, read them through as you would a novel or story. Don't skim them or read them quickly. Instead, read each one slowly as if it were a personal letter to you. Consider each book as if the author wrote it only for you. Make sure you have a

Bible commentary book handy and if anything is not clear to you, research the passage or thought. Also, keep a note pad near by and take notes as to what you learned and heard (internally from the Holy Spirit) as you read through each book. If you can do this with a friend, reading out loud to one another, then that is all the better. But remember, each time before you start to read, begin with a prayer and ask the Holy Spirit to come and tutor you. This experience will begin to answer many of your questions and therefore be very valuable. It will form a base foundation for all that you will encounter along the Road to Grace.

A Picture of the Road to Grace

The illustration on the following page illuminates a major but seldom considered fact: In life, we have but two paths to choose.[4]

If we follow the Way of the World—the road most people take—it will ultimately lead us to our destruction. Matthew 7:13-14, as shown in the picture, makes that point very clear. But if we choose the Road to Grace—the harder road to travel—we will ultimately find the gift of eternal life.

It is very difficult for us to believe that there could be so few choices on a matter that is so important. And there are many who will avoid or delay choosing the Road to Grace because it seems too difficult or radical a path to take. So instead we continue along our present course thinking that a more reasonable option will present itself sooner or later. We may feel like we are not making a choice and that we have time to do so, but in fact we have chosen to stay on the way of the world, a very unsafe place to be. This puts us in the same deadly position as the prodigal son who lived a life of sin when he was away from his father.

Scripture tells us that there are very definite consequences to our actions and thoughts. In Romans 6:23, we learn that as sinners we deserve death in the afterlife. Sin is literally anything that is not in agreement with God's Word or instruction—

Matthew 7:13-14

"Enter through the narrow gate; for the gate is wide and the road is easy that leads to destruction, and there are many who take it. For the gate is narrow and the road is hard that leads to life, and there are few who find it."

Eternal Life
A Gift from God
SERVE HIM
LOVE HIM
KNOW HIM
ROMANS 6:23
"For the wages of sin is death, but
the free gift of God is eternal life
in Christ Jesus our Lord."

whether we act improperly (sinfully) or when we fail to take the proper action (for example, excluding God from our every day lives). This is how people live as they walk along the Way of the World. It is especially hard for Catholics to believe that God considers all of us sinners at heart. Over the years, I think many of us have just come to believe that if we just go to church regularly, it will cover a multitude of sins. Additionally, we've always had the concept of venial sin to fall back on. It's born of the notion that God will tolerate some sin, the small, rather insignificant minor infractions that can bother God, but it will not condemn us to hell.

I strongly advise against this line of reasoning because it is a slippery slope. Remember this, venial sins can easily lead to mortal sins and because the activity that leads to the more grievous sin was minor in nature, we are likely to classify the larger sin as inconsequential as well. Saint Paul tells us that we are all sinners,

> *For there is no distinction, since* ***all have sinned*** *and fall short of the glory of God.*
>
> ROMANS 3:22-23, emphasis added

As Poor Catholics and make-believers, we and many others can all too easily find ourselves on the path that will ultimately lead to eternal death and separation from God. This is the part of the picture that many of us just cannot believe. Sure, we know that we're probably not perfect models of the "good Catholic," but we also reason that we certainly are not bad enough to merit the Lake of Fire. And there is our error. We use our reasoning, not God's. Again, this is a most important example of why we need to know and understand God's Word. Are we bad enough to deserve death in the Lake of Fire? If you feel you are not, then just think about your behavior each day.

How many times a day do you think about God, His Ten Commandments, the two Great Commandments and so on? How often do you pray to Him? How often do you offend Him in a day? Are you even aware that you offend Him? While we still bear the burden of Adam's original sin, we've added enough of our own transgressions to condemn us. Think about the following passages:

...As it is written: "There is no one who is righteous, not even one; there is no one who has understanding, there is no one who seeks God. All have turned aside, together they have become worthless; there is no one who shows kindness, there is not even one. Their throats are opened graves; they use their tongues to deceive. The venom of vipers is under their lips. Their mouths are full of cursing and bitterness. Their feet are swift to shed blood; ruin and misery are in their paths, and the way of peace they have not known. There is no fear of God before their eyes."

ROMANS 3:10-18

For many live as enemies of the cross of Christ; I have often told you of them, and now I tell you even with tears. Their end is destruction; their god is the belly; and their glory is in their shame; their minds are set on earthly things.

PHILIPPIANS 3:18-19

For it is indeed just of God to repay with affliction those who afflict you, and to give relief to the afflicted as well as to us, when the Lord Jesus is revealed from heaven with his mighty angels in flaming fire, inflicting vengeance on those who do not know God and on those who do not obey the gospel of our Lord Jesus. These will suffer the punishment of eternal destruction, separated from the presence of the Lord and from the glory of his might...

2 THESSALONIANS 1:6-9

Saint Paul makes it very clear that the sin that condemns us is our own sin; it is of our own doing. We've personally committed it, so we own it.

But because of Christ's sacrifice on the cross, we can find our way to eternal life. If it wasn't for Jesus, that option wouldn't exist for us. Jesus created the alternate route, the Road to Grace. But we must make the conscious decision to take that route. We must turn from the sin laden path we currently are on and steer onto the "road that leads to life." We have to trust Christ and choose His path. Personally, I'm very happy that there is one.

As consumers, however, many of us may feel that there should be a greater number of ways into the Kingdom. But there isn't. There is only one, Jesus Christ. He is the only bridge. This is one of the most central core beliefs of our Catholic faith. There's no alternative understanding or interpretation of this concept; you either believe it or you don't. The following Bible passages bear this out:

So again Jesus said to them, "Very truly, I tell you, I am the gate for the sheep."

JOHN 10:7

I am the gate. Whoever enters by me will be saved, and will come in and go out and find pasture.

JOHN 10:9

Jesus said to him, "I am the way, and the truth, and the life. No one comes to the Father except through me."

JOHN 14:6

This one point will test your most fundamental belief in God as a Catholic. It's a good example of how important it is to either believe in God's Word as presented in Scripture or not. There is no middle ground on this issue.

Our job is not only to get ourselves onto the Road to Grace, but also to help others on the Way of the World to see this alternative path we've chosen. As Jesus instructed, this is all part of the Great Commission:

Go therefore and make disciples of all nations, baptizing them in the name of the Father and of the Son and of the Holy Spirit, and teaching them to obey everything that I have commanded you. And remember, I am with you always, to the end of the age.

MATTHEW 28:19-20

As Catholics, we have to live our lives in such a way that others will be intrigued and interested in joining us along this alternative path. But the path is not without its dangers. As you can see in the picture, the bridge to eternal life is open at both ends. We can go and come as we please. God does not restrict us. As we find Christ to be real, we come back over the bridge, returning to the way of the world to help enlighten others. But in many cases, we can succumb to worldly temptations and end up living a life somewhere between a true Christian and a non-believer. We become make-believers.

Can you picture it? Some of us are constantly going back and forth over the bridge. We fail to remain on the path God tells us to follow. Consequently, we may sound godly in our speech, but our actions are quite worldly. It becomes difficult to see the real difference between us and people who don't know and follow Christ (another major complaint about Christians). And there is a difference, a big difference. We who know the Lord are not better than anyone else but we should be different in how we think and act. The best way to describe the difference is that we now see the world as God sees it.

Imagine this. If you were sitting near God and He was talking to you, He would be revealing things that only He knows. He might show you the whole picture of past history, the present and most importantly, what's to come in the future. Your eyes would be opened to much more than you already know and your opinion on many topics would probably change. This would cause you to think and act differently. As Catholics, this is exactly what is suppose to happen to us when we come to know the Lord. Because of our relationship with God, He reveals many new things to us. The following Bible passage about Lazarus demonstrates how important it is for us to have our eyes opened to Christ.

There was a rich man who was dressed in purple and fine linen and who feasted sumptuously every day. And at his gate lay a poor man named Lazarus, covered with sores, who longed to satisfy his hunger with what fell from the rich man's table; even the dogs would come and lick his sores. The poor man died and was carried away by the angels to be with Abraham. The rich man also died and was buried. In Hades, where he was being tormented, he looked up and saw Abraham far away with Lazarus by his side. He called out, "Father Abraham, have mercy on me, and send Lazarus to dip the tip of his finger in water and cool my tongue; for I am in agony in these flames." But Abraham said, "Child, remember that during your lifetime you received your good things, and Lazarus in like manner evil things; but now he is comforted here, and you are in agony. Besides all this, between you and us a great chasm has been fixed, so that those who might want to pass from here to you cannot do so, and no one can cross from there to us." He said, "Then, father, I beg you to send him to my father's house—for I have five brothers—that he may warn them, so that they will not also come into this place of torment." Abraham replied, "They have Moses and the prophets; they should listen to them." He said, "No, father Abraham; but if someone goes to them from the dead, they will repent." He said to him, "If they do not listen to Moses and the prophets, neither will they be convinced even if someone rises from the dead."

LUKE 16:19-31

When Lazarus saw the truth of what was happening, He wanted to act differently toward his brothers and sisters. But it was too late. We as Christians have been awakened to the same truth. We see things that others cannot, not because we're smarter or better, but because we asked God to show us, and He does. This changes us and we now feel a great need to alert others to the truth of what we see. Like Lazarus, we change and become different, altered by the experience. But unlike Lazarus, we still have the opportunity to make changes in our own lives. So yes, we are very different. Meeting Jesus will do that to you.

Just finding the Road to Grace doesn't mean that you are home free. You have to stay on that road and walk and sometimes even climb your way home. That's why Saint Paul told us to,

...work out your own salvation with fear and trembling.

PHILIPPIANS 2:12

A further threat to us on this road is that we might even return permanently to the way of the world. It's called backsliding, permanently regressing into our old ways. We can literally return to our old sinful habits. A good example of this condition is when an alcoholic who was making good progress against his or her addiction goes back to drinking heavily. The question then becomes if they will ever try to beat the addiction again. It remains to be seen. With God's help all things are possible. We each have until the very last breath we draw to return to God. Each of us has that same wonderful opportunity with Christ.

But Saint Peter had a stern warning for people who have come to know God but either choose to return to a life of sin or secretly maintain their sinful habits:

For if, after they have escaped the defilements of the world through the knowledge of our Lord and Savior Jesus Christ, they are again entangled in them and overpowered, the last state has become worse for them than the first. For it would have been better for them never to have known the way of righteousness than, after knowing it, to turn back from the holy commandment that was passed on to them. It has happened to them according to the true proverb, "The dog turns back to its own vomit," and, "The sow is washed only to wallow in the mud."

2 PETER 2:20-22

On either path, The Way of the World or the Road to Grace, we keep our free will throughout our lives. You end up on either road by your own choice and no one else's.

But as soon as we step onto the Road to Grace we begin immediately to learn about God. Our knowledge of Him starts to grow and develop. If we faithfully remain on that path, our love for Him grows and a desire to serve Him surfaces. Again we hear Jesus' words of prayer to His Father in John 17:3, pointing us toward the bridge to life:

And this is eternal life, that they may know you, the only true God, and Jesus Christ whom you have sent.

JOHN 17:3

This is the path Jesus wants us to take. He wants us to come to know the Father. In the end, it will lead us to God's gift of eternal life. Remember the following quote from Matthew 7:21:

Not everyone who says to me, "Lord, Lord," will enter the kingdom of heaven, but only the one who does the will of my Father in heaven.

MATTHEW 7:21

Its lesson reverberates throughout this whole picture. Only the people who have developed an intimate knowledge and love for God will find eternal life.

Finally, the Road to Grace illustration brings up one particular criticism of Catholicism which is its seeming preoccupation with hell and the threat it poses. But it's worth noting that the Catholic Church did not invent the concept of hell. Jesus Himself spoke often about it, as did the writers of the Old Testament. To ignore its reality would be spiritual suicide. Read the following verses.

...and anyone whose name was not found written in the book of life was thrown into the lake of fire.

REVELATION 20:15

In the path of righteousness there is life, in walking its path there is no death.

PROVERBS 12:28

But as for the cowardly, the faithless, the polluted, the murderers, the fornicators, the sorcerers, the idolaters, and all liars, their place will be in the lake that burns with fire and sulfur, which is the second death.

Revelation 21:8

Over the years of training as an accountant and auditor, I was always taught to be realistic and practical. Ignoring facts that might turn out to be important later on could lead to failure or even disaster. The Scriptures make it clear that there is a place known as hell and the way of the world does lead to death and destruction. It is not pleasant to think about, but it is real and so we must face it head on.

It is a natural human response to think that all of this does not apply to us personally. We may think that it only applies to those people who have long worked at being enemies of God. But again a careful reading and study of the Scriptures on this topic will show us otherwise. Again, the choice is ours.

How then, does someone get onto the Road to Grace?

In answer to that question, I have developed a short practical program of steps that we as Catholics and Christians can follow to build a walking faith with God once we step onto the Road to Grace. These steps lead to a door through which God will reveal a knowledge of Himself, a desire to return His love to Him and a desire to serve Him—and ultimately bring us home to Him in heaven. As you work through these steps, take your time between and during each step. This cannot be rushed. Take the first step and then see how God responds to you.

Three Steps Toward Salvation Along the Road to Grace

Step 1: Coming to know God

And this is eternal life, that they may know you, the only true God, and Jesus Christ whom you have sent.

JOHN 17:3

Coming to know God is the most critical step on the Road to Grace. Once we begin to look for Him, He will reveal Himself to us in a manner and at a pace that we can accept. Focus here on your goal, which is to find out all you can about God. Sometimes the easiest way to study a topic is to answer the simple questions of who, what, where, when, why and how. The answers to these questions can be quite extensive.

Action Plan A

- Start seeking God in all of your prayers. Talk to Him as you would a friend whenever you remember to pray. Do this especially when you rise every morning. It is how you should start the day with Him.
- Read the Scriptures. Start with the four Gospels and concentrate on what God reveals about Himself in whatever verses you read. Be sure to follow the cross references (make sure you use a Bible that has this feature) back to the Old Testament as well. Another good place to start is with the Bible verses (many of which are core Scriptures) I've cited in this book. Research each one until you are sure you understand it. And certainly, if you can find a Bible study to join, go and listen to what is being discussed. But remember, take nothing that you hear for granted. Always check it out for yourself and see if you can find it in the Scriptures and in the catechism.

Action Plan B

- Prepare yourself, through prayer, to make the most significant Act of Contrition of your entire life. When you are ready, ask God to help you say the prayer. Take your time to make sure you've covered all the areas of sin in your life as best you can remember. Also consider the things you want to change for good. If you have a prayer partner, spouse or close friend, consider sharing this prayer with them as you go through it. Make sure you go to Confession soon thereafter to confirm your Act of Contrition.
- Next, when you are ready, ask God to come into your heart and lead you through the rest of your life. Literally dedicate

yourself to Him and everything He represents. Resolve to become an ambassador for Christ. Accept His gift of eternal life. Concentrate your prayer on John 17:3, the key Scripture cited above.

Tip: Keep a journal of what you say to God in the form of a prayer. There are a number of ways to do this. You can start a prayer journal (which I highly recommend) similar to the one I described earlier in the book. You can also keep record in a journal by event or meeting. For example, every time you have a Bible Study meeting (use two or three pages per meeting), make notes of major points you learned and thoughts and actions you want to pursue. Highlight each one and return frequently to each page and chart your progress.

Step 2: Coming to Love God

So we have known and believe the love that God has for us.
God is love, and those who abide in love abide in God, and God abides in them.

1 JOHN 4:16

In Step 1, you are mostly gathering information and knowledge about God. As you do, you should be sensing a growing passion for the things of God. Things that matter to Him, as revealed in the Scriptures, should start being of concern to you. Don't miss the incredibly important statement that God is love. Everything we talked about in this book, as well as the Bible, is built on this premise. Now it must become the very foundation for all that you will learn and do for God.

Action Plan A

• Continue to pray that God will help you develop a greater love not only for Him but also for those around you. Ask Him to help you demonstrate that love to others, especially at home and work. Ask your prayer partner(s) to pray for you in this endeavor. Then put your prayers into action by doing something small, loving and totally unexpected for someone you work or live with. Some call this activity a "random act of kindness." It's the beginning of forming a habit of doing good things for others.

Action Plan B

• Look for a small group to help you as you move along on this part of your walk with God. Perhaps members of the Bible study you attend would be interested in working with you on building their love for God and others. Having a small group of people who are also trying to accomplish what you are doing, will benefit you with invaluable encouragement and sharing. If you have the time, this would be a good opportunity to volunteer to help serve the needy either through your Church or some other program. Begin slowly at this point and don't let anything discouraging stop you. Take small steps and do not over-commit yourself.

Tip: Add those who need special prayers and help to your prayer journal. Dedicate at least one page per person and chart their progress. If there are many people, then a separate prayer journal is advised. Make a list of your prayers and the answers with dates. You'll be amazed at what you see over time.

Step 3: Coming To Serve God

And the king will answer them, "Truly I tell you, just as you did it to one of the least of these who are members of my family, you did it to me."

Matthew 25:40

This is where your faith becomes visible through your works. God's grace has been working in you throughout Step 1 and Step 2, preparing you not only internally in building your faith, but also externally, so that you will naturally want to do more for those around you. Saint John gives us a wonderful example of this in the life of Jesus:

Now before the festival of the Passover, Jesus knew that his hour had come to depart from this world and go to the Father. Having loved his own who were in the world, he loved them to the end. The devil had already put it into the heart of Judas son of Simon Iscariot to betray him. And during supper Jesus, knowing that the Father had given all things into his hands, and that he had come from God and was going to God, got up from the table, took off his outer robe, and tied a towel around himself. Then he poured water into a basin and began to wash the disciples' feet and to wipe them with the towel that was tied around him.

JOHN 13:1-5

Whatever situations in life you encounter along your walk, try to always first ask yourself, "What would Jesus Do?" Your newfound knowledge and love for God should influence your mind and will and suggest what action is appropriate for you to take under the circumstances. But always use God as your reference point. Imagine Him being with you wherever you go. He'll be right there next to you. Lean into Him for everything. Ask Him for what you need and rely on His wisdom.

Action Plan A

- You now need to learn how your behavior should mature in Christ. Reading the Gospels of how Christ responded to various situations will help you. You may also wish to emulate some of the actions of other people you know who spend their time helping others. But know your limits and whenever possible, take another person with you when you go to help someone (go out two by two, just as Jesus sent out His Disciples).

• Also read the commentaries (such as The Collegeville Bible Commentary) which will explain in detail, the motives behind Jesus' actions. This will help you respond more positively to peoples' needs. It's easy to get discouraged in this kind of work. There are a lot of people with serious needs. Keeping a strong sense of purpose and knowing how Jesus responded to people will help you overcome any disappointment.

• Follow in Jesus' steps. This may sound impossible, but the more you study how He lived and acted in given situations, the easier it becomes to know how to act and think like Jesus. Again, whenever you come up against a tough decision, start formulating an answer by asking the question, "What would Jesus do?" Then over time, graduate to, "What *did* Jesus do?" It's easier to train yourself in this technique on the simpler questions first. So start slowly. As you serve more and more people in their needs, finding answers to the bigger problems will become more challenging. Just remember to lean on the Lord.

Action Plan B

• Serving God is not exclusive to Step 3; it should be part of all you do along the Road to Grace. Remember that wherever you are on this Road, your goal is to always know God in everything, to always react to those around you with love and to serve those in need as if they themselves were Jesus Christ. Most important of all is that in everything we do, we should always bring glory to God. We must never, ever place ourselves in God's position of receiving the glory. He deserves all the praise, thanksgiving and congratulations for any successes in answered prayers. We are simply His messengers and channels for His grace.

• As you proceed on the Road to Grace, think of yourself as being blind with God as your guide. Without Him you can do nothing. Jesus always submitted to His Father in all things. We too need to submit to Christ in all that we do. In that way our success will be guaranteed.

Tip: Again it is good to keep a journal of those special situations where you've served God and others. You'll develop an incredible book of memories and testimonies.

Some Additional Thoughts

In today's culture, we are quick to make up lists of things we need to accomplish each day. The Three Steps Toward Salvation listed above might easily be seen as something that could be done as part of a "to do" list. It would be a great mistake to try and accomplish this most important journey in such a mechanical manner. These three steps are how you develop a close relationship with God. If it were simply up to us, we could not even begin to achieve anything like this. The only reason we can attempt this process is because God wants us to succeed and therefore we can succeed in this effort. He makes Himself available to us, so we can know Him, love Him and serve Him. I remember what someone once said, "Religion is man's attempt at reaching God. Christianity is God's attempt at reaching man." This plan demonstrates the truth of this statement—which brings us to another important thought.

During this three-step journey, we need to always remember that we are attempting to come to know a supernatural creature. God is far above us in all aspects and capacities. We can only begin to understand Him as He discloses certain aspects of Himself to us. Again this is further proof of God's desire to have a close personal relationship with us. If He didn't want this, there would be no way we could even begin to approach Him for any purpose. The fact that we are allowed to go to Him, proves His desire for closeness. Oswald Chambers in his book, *My Utmost for His Highest*, makes the following three observations: [3]

Knowing God

If a person wants scientific knowledge, then intellectual curiosity must be his guide. But if he desires knowledge and insight into the teachings of Jesus Christ, he can only obtain it through obedience. If spiritual things seem dark and hidden to me, then I can be sure that there is a point of disobedience somewhere in my life. (July 27 entry)

Loving God

Have you ever been driven to do something for God not because you felt that it was useful or your duty to do so, or that there was anything in it for you, but simply because you love Him? Have you ever realized that you can give things to God that are of value to Him? Or are you just sitting around daydreaming about the greatness of His redemption, while neglecting all the things you could be doing for Him? I'm not referring to works which could be regarded as divine and miraculous, but ordinary, simple human things—things which would be evidence to God that you are totally surrendered to Him. Have you ever created what Mary of Bethany created in the heart of the Lord Jesus? "She has done a good work for Me" (Mark 14:6). (February 21 entry)

Serving God

Never run before God gives you His direction. If you have the slightest doubt, then He is not guiding. Whenever there is doubt—wait. Peter did not wait for God. He predicted in his own mind where the test would come, and it came where he did not expect it. "I will lay down my life for Your sake." Peter's statement was honest but ignorant. "Jesus answered him, '...the rooster shall not crow till you have denied Me three times.'" (John 13:38). Natural devotion may be enough to attract us to Jesus... but it will never make us disciples. Natural devotion will deny Jesus, always falling short of what it means to truly follow Him.

(January 4 entry)

Chambers is telling us that if we want to know God, a supernatural creature, then obedience is the key. God tests our sincerity in asking to know Him, by seeing if we will become obedient to His ways. As soon as we balk at complying to His laws, it stops the process of getting closer to Him. Until we comply on a given point, He will keep presenting us with that same issue until we understand that we must yield our will to His.

Recall our discussion about the three levels of belief. It's the same issue here. Knowing God occurs on three levels. I can read many articles, books and Scripture verses that talk about God. It would give me a great deal of "head knowledge" about Him. But I wouldn't know Him, I'd only know of Him.

Yet it was the knowledge growth and the obedience to His will that first enabled me to start along the Road to Grace. The more you obey Him, even in the small things, the more God reveals of Himself to you, the greater will be your understanding of Him and the things you're involved in.

Chambers goes on to instruct us how to truly love God; we need to be like Mary of Bethany (see Mark 14:3-9). The good news here is that we can do things for Christ that He will personally appreciate. When you love someone, even a supernatural being, you will want to express that love. But those who are truly in love will want to find a form of expression for that love that will get to the heart of their loved one. And this leads us to the final step.

Chambers alerts us to a very common mistake of those in love with Jesus; they rush out to start their good works before hearing specific instructions from God. When we do this, we will fail and the failure can be as bitter as it was to Peter that night he denied Christ, his one true love.

If you have read this far in the book, then your reward is this: No matter who you are or what you have done, God is willing to open himself up to you and allow you to become a part of him and to enjoy His greatness. You can know Him, love Him and serve Him and be happy with Him in heaven, forever. This life is short, we know that all too well; and then what? Start looking for an eternal return on your spiritual efforts. Being Catholics, we are blessed with the opportunity of being able to begin accessing the rewards of an eternal life with God, here and now. We don't have to wait until Judgment Day. Accessing God now also helps assure us of a future with Him. The Last Day will not be a threat to us. It will be a day of rejoicing.

Start with the Three Steps Toward Salvation Along The Road to Grace. Your walk is toward something you have never even imagined. Your life will change once and for all. And you will begin to touch the new life that awaits you in heaven. You can begin to taste it now.

24

Closing Thoughts

I believe we have, to a certain extent, some control over when we depart this earth. If we commit to work for Him, He will use us. Then, when we have gone as far as He wants and as far as we can, He'll call us home. Similarly, the key to true success in this life depends upon where we place our greatest efforts. If we look to build up earthly wealth, then when we pass away, we will lose all of it. This kind of success is temporary like our lives. But if we build up wealth that follows us to the next life, then that is permanent and forever (see Luke 12:33).

I remember hearing a great truth from an unlikely source. Thomas S. Haggai, chairman and president of IGA, Inc., cleverly said, "Oh God, don't let me die until I'm dead." Mr. Haggai, a deeply spiritual man, discovered the truth about Jesus Christ. He realized that while his work was very important, there was something even more critical that needed expression, his love for God. I am surmising that he made his plea because his love for God was strong and he wanted the maximum time on earth to express that love. He wanted to effectively spread the Gospel for Christ thereby building up true treasure in heaven. So here was someone deeply involved in the world of business who came to know, love and serve God. It's a fine example for all of us to emulate.

There is much to do in serving the Lord. But as we move faster and faster in our normal daily routines, we become less and less likely of having success in God's work because God's work takes time and patience. Jesus Himself modeled this for us, walking without haste or anxiousness throughout His entire ministry. If we continue to physically and mentally move faster and faster, our use to God becomes more and more limited. When we don't know how to slow down, we are less able to invest ourselves in those who need us.

This reminds me of the nuns I had as teachers back in grammar school. When they gave us exams, they always timed us, saying very loudly at the end of a test, "Time's up, pencils down!" I always needed just two or three minutes more to finish up, but never received the extra time. We can't count on getting extra time in life, either. Sadly, too many of us will realize this truth only when it's too late to do anything about it.

People have asked me how I came up with this book's title. Read carefully the following passage—one of the key Scriptures of this book—and you'll see not only the derivation of the title, but also what God said about the make-believers:

I know your works; you are neither cold nor hot. I wish that you were either cold or hot. So, because you are lukewarm, and neither cold nor hot, I am about to spit you out of my mouth. For you say, "I am rich, I have prospered, and I need nothing." You do not realize that you are wretched, pitiable, poor, blind, and naked. Therefore I counsel you to buy from me gold refined by fire so that you may be rich; and white robes to clothe you and to keep the shame of your nakedness from being seen; and salve to anoint your eyes so that you may see. I reprove and discipline those whom I love. Be earnest, therefore, and repent.

REVELATION 3:15-19

Through Saint John, God spoke to the Church in Laodicea, a wealthy industrial center of its day. Besides having a renowned medical school, it was also a major banking and finance capital of the region.

Its key exports were fine woolen garments and an eye salve sought by many. It was so wealthy that after a devastating earthquake of A.D. 60/61, the residents were able to totally rebuild the city with their own funds. Yet the hearts of these people had become hardened and self-satisfied. These believers would not take a committed position on anything. Their indifference toward others and important issues of the day had led them into a place where they neglected to do much of anything for Christ. At best they were following God only half-heartedly. In the above passage, God is telling these people that to be lukewarm is the worst possible way to live. Additionally, their wealth gave them a false sense of security, which led to an attitude of complacency and indifference. Money dulled their spiritual desire for the things of God and now they were in real trouble with Him.

When Christ tells the Laodiceans to buy their gold from Him, He is exhorting them to build up spiritual treasures, which would last in heaven (see also Matthew 6:19-21, where Jesus talks about real treasures and where our hearts are). The reference to white garments was His appeal to them to become righteous (morally correct) in their actions and thoughts. He wanted them to return to living honorable lives and being pure in their dealings with one another. He also advised them to seek God's medicine to open their eyes to see the truth about Christ (see also John 9:39).

The Laodiceans had lost their way and no longer saw Jesus as the way to eternal life. And in just one quote from the Holy Scriptures, we can see the wisdom of God's desires for us today. He's telling us plainly that all of our wealth and possessions are meaningless without a right relationship with God. And He says that He will correct and discipline those He cares about, just as we do with our children when they act improperly. So it is reasonable for us to expect a little correction from time to time as we move along the Road to Grace. But, read the very next verse. Yet again, what Jesus wants most from us comes shining through:

Listen! I am standing at the door, knocking; if you hear my voice and open the door, I will come in to you and eat with you, and you with me.

REVELATION 3:20

There's a popular painting of this particular verse. In it, Jesus is depicted knocking on a large, well-built door waiting for someone to answer. There's no handle or latch on His side of the door; it can only be opened from the inside. The message is clear: Jesus can come to us in a very personal way but, only if we let Him in. So, my final, bottom line advice to you is this:

1. Make up your mind about Jesus Christ.

Decide once and for all, who He is and what He means to you. Do you believe in the God of the Bible or some other version of that God (remember the make-believers)? Do you even know what's in the Bible to help you make that decision? Research the Bible and catechism, make a choice (for Him, hopefully) and then follow that choice. If you do believe in Him, then start on the Road to Grace. Don't wait any longer. You've been away from "home" for too long and now time for you is very precious.

If you do not know or cannot decide about God, then you need to do some research. I've already cited the following two Scriptures earlier in our discussion. But I repeat them here only because they are so important for so many of us. Since we have so many options available to us today as to how we can gain eternal life, we must find out which one is true. Jesus made the claim that He's the only way into heaven. The problem is that if His claim is true then we must determine that for ourselves. Otherwise we will continue to go in "spiritual circles" for the rest of our lives and get nowhere. *So you must choose.* At this point, it's not a "we" thing. Each of us must make up his or her own mind about Christ.

Thomas said to him, "Lord, we do not know where you are going. How can we know the way?" Jesus said to him, "I am the way, and the truth, and the life. No one comes to the Father except through me. If you know me, you will know my Father also. From now on you do know him and have seen him."

JOHN 14:5-7

I am the gate. Whoever enters by me will be saved, and will come in and go out and find pasture.

JOHN 10:9

For sure, these are two of the most offensive verses in Scripture today because once again, they tell us that there's only one way into heaven and it's through Jesus Christ. This idea is totally against our contemporary consumerist culture, our modern sense of inclusiveness as being politically correct. It also reveals our sheer arrogance.

Many of us are convinced these two verses just cannot be right because if they are, then a very large number of people will never see heaven—to us an unthinkable and impossible prospect. Despite these verses and others like them throughout the Bible, our own gut feelings seem to tell us that there have to be many ways into heaven, just like there are many choices to other things in life. But if we cling to this notion, then it will represent the ultimate speculation; we will be gambling with our eternal lives. And if we are wrong, what then?

Look at it this way: Suppose you were convinced that you had five minutes left to live. What would you do? Would you pray? If so, to whom? At that moment, you will be in the same position as the two thieves on the cross. What will be your bet? Will you bet on Jesus being the one way in or not? Which thief represents you? If you would choose God at that point, then do it now. Acknowledge Him now while you still have the chance, because you never know when and how you'll meet your end. At that moment, you may not have the option of choosing. *Do not wait any longer!*

Seek the LORD while he may be found, call upon him while he is near.

ISAIAH 55:6

2. Don't let your religion stand in the way of your faith.

As Catholics, we've become very soft and flabby about our faith in God. We've let others take care of "all the details" for us. We have sat in our churches and listened to sermons and homilies for years. We've received Communion over and over. Some of us have even gone to Confession a number of times! Again, for some reason we Catholics think that this is enough. It is not. It is only a minimal beginning to our faith walk.

You may not agree with all that we have discussed in this book, but you must admit one thing: God wants us to know, love and serve Him. You can only begin to do this while sitting in a church. Jesus' Disciples sat in their "church" while listening to the Master's instructions (see Mark 4:33-34) and then they went out to where the people were. Our religious leaders can only do so much for us and God has been waiting for us to realize that we too are empowered to do His work.

It's time for each of us to go to Christ directly and then come back and serve our Church and the Body of Christ. When Jesus took some of His Disciples up on a mountain for the Transfiguration, He resisted the temptation to remain up there, where it was magnificent and He was in His glory. He returned to the valley where He was needed. We too need to go where God needs us. We can't let anything stand in our way in answering God's call. But we first need to go to Him personally and start on the Road to Grace. There is no other way.

Remember my catechism story. God made us to know, love and serve Him in this world and to be happy with Him in the next. If we live the first part of that sentence—if we come to know God—then the second, third and fourth part will follow. Go to Him, now.

3. Remember: You already have the ability to make the changes you need to make.

If you've read this far and still aren't persuaded about the choice you'll have to make, then let's look at this from another angle. Many Christians know and agree that time as we know it will reach a last day when God will sit in judgment over each one of us. This judgment will happen and we will all be there.

Now, "fast forward" to that very day. Picture all of us standing together on an incredibly vast plain, waiting for God to begin His judgment. What do you think people are most concerned about at this moment? They are wondering how God is going to judge us and they want to know what the criteria will be. Scripture has already given us the answer:

For it is indeed just of God to repay with affliction those who afflict you, and to give relief to the afflicted as well as to us, when the Lord Jesus is revealed from heaven with his mighty angels in flaming fire, inflicting vengeance on those who do not know God and on those who do not obey the gospel of our Lord Jesus. These will suffer the punishment of eternal destruction, separated from the presence of the Lord and from the glory of his might…

2 THESSALONIANS 1:6-9

Not everyone who says to me, "Lord, Lord," will enter the kingdom of heaven, ***but only the one who does the will of my Father in heaven.***

MATTHEW 7:21, emphasis added

Again, if you read the very literal account in Matthew 25 of how God will judge us on the last day, you see only two groups of people:

All the nations will be gathered before him, and he will separate people one from another as a shepherd separates the sheep from the goats, and he will put the sheep at his right hand and the goats at the left. Then the king will say to those at his right hand, "Come, you that are blessed by my Father, inherit the kingdom prepared for you from the foundation of the world…"

Then he will say to those at his left hand, "You that are accursed, depart from me into the eternal fire prepared for the devil and his angels…"

MATTHEW 25:32-34, 41

Those God saves will be the ones who cared for those in need and who showed love for those near them. The criteria is really quite simple, is it not? Again, my friends, it all comes down to only two choices. Whom do we choose to follow—God or the world?

Enter through the narrow gate; for the gate is wide and the road is easy that leads to destruction, and there are many who take it. For the gate is narrow and the road is hard that leads to life, and there are few who find it.

MATTHEW 7:13-14

Nothing worth achieving comes easily. The gate and road to heaven are narrow and difficult because they demand that we overcome our natural, human tendency to want the easy way, the short cut. But there is none here. As shown in the picture of the Road to Grace earlier, if you follow the crowds taking the path of least resistance, then you're most probably headed for the worst result.

I've been told that at times I may be too tenacious and don't know when to give up. And maybe this is one of those times. But if you still cannot make up your mind whether to follow Christ and develop a close walking faith with God—or you've simply decided not to follow Him, then right now you need to hope that:

- Everything in the Bible is false.
- None of the people mentioned in the Bible were real and the stories about them never really happened.
- Jesus, even though His existence, words and deeds have been historically verified, did not say and do the things as recorded in Scripture and history.
- All the Disciples and Saints who were martyred over the last 2,000 years, believed in God as a myth or fable and died for nothing.
- All the popes, cardinals, bishops and clergy who ever lived (of all Christian churches) were 100% wrong about their beliefs in God.

Finally, you need to hope that the millions upon millions of people, who have decided to live as Christians and followers of God since the beginning of time, were and are all wrong and have essentially chosen to believe in a myth. And finally, when you do face God on that last day, you need to hope beyond all hope that He will not do to you what He said He would do to those who did not live their lives believing in Him and the One whom He sent, Jesus Christ.

Now, having said all of that (and fully believing that it is true), allow me to give you some supportive thoughts as I close this book. Since page one, we have become familiar with someone lovingly known as "the Poor Catholic." Throughout the discussion, he or she appears to be a person who has lost his or her way home to God. The core of the problem is that instead of realizing it's God's will that must be complied with, the poor Catholic has been convinced (by the culture) that it's okay to have things his or her way virtually all the time. The result is someone who is poor indeed because they have exchanged God's ways and love for the ways and lure of our culture.

We've learned that the penalty for this is truly severe. It produces a great deal of pain for us in this life and includes the worst thing, eternal separation from God. But I have come to learn that the threat of hell and separation from God is a totally unnecessary occurrence and we need not live in fear of it. Perhaps this is the most overlooked part of the Good News of Christ's Gospel. Jesus died so that we would not have to go to hell when we die. I believe that if any one of us ends up in hell, it's because we wanted to go there and worked very hard to get there! Hell is a place we go to by choice.

Once I realized that God was indeed real, I sought after Him and found Him. My discovery convinced me that since God is real, then hell must also be real. This event put me to work developing my knowledge of Him, my love for Him and my service to Him. It has even produced this book. I progressed in my walk with Him to the point where I am no longer preoccupied with thoughts of hell, eternal separation from God or even indecision as to whether there is a hell or not. I decided to end all of that uncertainty by making a decision. I have made my choice and it is *for* Jesus. This has given me a peace in my life and consequently, I can rest easy in my concern for my personal disposition after death.

However, I now have taken on the task of seeing things as God sees them. Even though I can only see a tiny part of what He sees, still it staggers me. My chief concern is to help others see what God knows to be true about their future. These facts have weighed heavily on me not because of the enormous opportunities and dangers they present, but rather at how blind and deaf we have become to the truth of Jesus Christ. He is the answer to so many of our problems. As Catholics, we could do so much to help ourselves and others if we would just live as real Catholics. Modeling the life Christ taught us to live would encourage others, who desperately need real purpose in life, to join us in our faith.

We need Jesus. There is no other way to heaven, so stop wasting your time looking for one. And stop worrying about whether or not you'll make it into heaven or purgatory. Get rid of all your doubt and make a choice for Christ and do it now. Remember, we have one major supporter, Jesus Himself. He wants us all to come home, *all of us.*

> *And this is the will of him who sent me, that I should lose nothing of all that he has given me, but raise it up on the last day.*
>
> JOHN 6:39

Get onto the Road to Grace now. Do not hesitate any longer. It's time to turn and start the walk back home to be with your Father. When you get within sight of Him, you'll find that He's been patiently waiting for you to return all these years. As He did with the prodigal son, He will open His arms wide and receive you with all of His love. Now's the time to return... nothing would make Him happier. Amen.

NOTES

1 Robinson, Haddon. This material is taken from *What Jesus Said About Successful Living* by Haddon Robinson. Copyright © 1991. Used by permission of Discovery House Publishers, Box 3566, Grand Rapids, Michigan 49501. All rights reserved.

2 Chambers, Oswald. Quotes are taken from *My Utmost for His Highest* by Oswald Chambers, edited by James Reimann. Copyright © 1992 by Oswald Chambers Publications Assn., Ltd. and is used by permission of Discovery House Publishers, Box 3566, Grand Rapids MI 49501. All rights reserved.

3 Barna, George. Quotes are taken from October 21, 2003 Barna Update, "Americans Describe their Views about Life After Death" and October 8, 2002, "Americans Draw Theological Beliefs from Diverse Points of View" as published by The Barna Group, 1957 Eastman Ave. Ste. B, Ventura, Calif. 93003.

4 Artwork by Timothy Lundgren, Torrington, Connecticut. www.timlundgren.com.

5 FCCI is also known as Christ@Work.

ACKNOWLEDGEMENTS

A book is never written and published solely by the efforts of the author. It is always a collaborative undertaking, whereby any number of people might be enlisted to help produce the work. And so it is with *The Poor Catholic.*

I am indebted to my good friends Jack and Linda Brady and Kathy Young, who have quietly supported me and worked behind the scenes in order to help put the pieces of the "publishing puzzle" together. Another group of people who helped make this book a reality are Gail Dell, Maura Shaw, Andy Petersen, Tim Lundgren, Shelly Angers, Nigel Mumford, Ron Dower and others who came along at very critical points in the book's development and provided something crucially important; they encouraged me, not just once but many times. I will always be thankful for that support. And then there were others along the way such as family members, who added critical words of advice and constructive criticism that helped mold and shape the work. They too share in my love and thanks.

But *The Poor Catholic* really started to be written over 33 years ago when my wife Marcia first met me and immediately started to pray for my salvation. She recognized then that I was the original "Poor Catholic" and knew I needed to know Christ personally. Her prayers were powerful enough to open the door for God to work in my life and His influence eventually produced a book such as this.

To Marcia I am grateful beyond words.

To my Lord and Savior, I am, and will forever be, thankful for all He has done for me.

ABOUT THE AUTHOR

Angelo Paul Ramunni grew up as a Catholic on Long Island, New York in the 1950's and 60's. He attended Catholic schools all throughout his formal educational career. After graduating from Fairfield University with a Bachelor's degree in Economics in 1970, he went on to earn a Master's Degree in Economics from Fordham University in 1972, and eventually a second Master's Degree in Accounting from Long Island University in 1976.

In 1978 Angelo became a Certified Public Accountant and started his own public accounting firm in 1982, of which he is still a partner. His work with clients both on a business and personal level, has led him to focus on larger issues concerning peoples' finances, such as how to best utilize their wealth in a manner that would please God. More and more he found himself talking to clients and friends about spiritual matters as he analyzed peoples' needs and concerns about their future. Much of that practical experience helped form the basis for *The Poor Catholic.*

Over the years, the author became very active in his Catholic church and other para-church ministries as well as civic groups such as the Lions Club and as a past president of a local Rotary International club. He personally facilitated many Bible studies, Christian Business Owners group meetings, taught seminars concerning the godly use of money for individuals and business owners, as well as teaching groups how to integrate their faith with their work. Angelo is an adjunct teacher at the University of Connecticut in the field of accounting and has been active as a director of a number of non-profit organizations as well as a director of a local mutual savings bank.

He lives in Canaan, Connecticut with his wife and best friend, Marcia and has two grown children, Daniel and Joy.

For additional materials and resources, please visit our website at

www.thepoorcatholic.com